D1086055

Louisiana Security Devices

Louisiana Security Devices

A Précis

SECOND EDITION

Jason J. Kilborn

CAROLINA ACADEMIC PRESS

Durham, North Carolina

Library of Congress Cataloging-in-Publication Data

Kilborn, Jason J.
Louisiana security devices : a precis / Jason J. Kilborn. -- 2nd ed.
  p. cm.
Includes bibliographical references and index.
ISBN 978-1-61163-183-8 (alk. paper)
1. Security (Law)--Louisiana. I. Title.

KFL175.K55 2012
346.76307'4--dc23

2012002154

CAROLINA ACADEMIC PRESS

700 Kent Street
Durham, North Carolina 27701
Telephone (919) 489-7486
Fax (919) 493-5668
www.cap-press.com

Printed in the United States of America.

To Randy Trahan, Alain Levasseur, and Mike Rubin, who inspired me to learn about the Civil Law and who taught me everything I know about how it intersects with modern commercial law

Contents

Preface

This book is designed to demystify the complex and multifaceted law of secured transactions in Louisiana. One can easily get lost in the myriad of details of any one aspect of this law. This book is intended to serve as a map. The historically complex law of security devices has been further complicated by Louisiana's adoption of Article 9 of the Uniform Commercial Code (including the most recent revision in 2001), replete with non-uniform modifications to fit Louisiana's unique legal and commercial environment. Especially when one attempts to chart the boundaries and overlap among security interests, mortgages, and statutory privileges in provisions in the Civil Code, Code Ancillaries, and Chapter 9 of Title 10 of the Revised Statutes (the Louisiana Commercial Laws), clear guidance is virtually nonexistent. This book attempts to fill that void and offer an overview of the new world of Louisiana security devices in the 21st century.

The title of this book reflects its carefully confined goal, however. This is not a "treatise," so the reader will not find every answer to every question, nor even an analysis of each provision of this area of the law and illustrative jurisprudence. Instead, in this "précis," one will find a basic exposition of the main ideas and most commonly encountered provisions in modern secured transactions law. To be sure, this book is designed to answer many—perhaps most—questions that will occur to the average student, practitioner, or researcher in this area. Even for those questions left unanswered, this book should set even the most unseasoned novice on the right track to finding the answer elsewhere, if need be.

The intended audience for this book thus ranges from the student wading through the material in a Security Devices or Secured Credit or Secured Transactions course, to the new lawyer setting out on a confusing research assignment in a case involving a secured transaction, to the experienced lawyer returning to this area of the law after an extended absence to find that the law has changed dramatically in the past 15, 10, and even 5 years. In writing this book, I hope to ease the lives of many such people by reducing their research time for a complex secured transaction project from days to hours (or from hours to minutes) and increasing their confidence in the solution to sometimes very difficult problems.

Jason Kilborn
Baton Rouge, LA

Introduction

What Is a Security Device and Why Do They Exist?

A "security device" is a statutory or contractual mechanism that enhances the likelihood that the person to whom an obligation is owed (the "obligee" or "creditor") will have a reliable and certain source of recovery of value if the person who owes the obligation (the "obligor" or "debtor") fails to live up to her end of the bargain (in other words, if she "defaults" on the obligation). A security device allows the creditor to feel more "secure" that an obligation will be met, particularly if the obligor has less-than-perfect creditworthiness. If the obligor fails to perform, a security device allows the creditor either to have identified items of the debtor's property seized and sold and the proceeds applied to the debt (in preference to the rights of other unpaid creditors), or to seek payment from some third party. Security devices are thus "accessory" to "principal obligations" that they support. One cannot have an effective security device without a principal obligation. In most secured transactions (that is, deals involving a security device), the principal obligation is to repay a sum of money previously lent by the creditor (often a bank), but security devices support many sorts of obligations to transfer value.

The availability of security devices encourages those with money to lend it to others to whom they might not lend without greater security of repayment. This increases economic activity (and, we hope, general welfare) by putting money to productive use in the flow of commerce. Encouraging people to enter into transactions and create societally beneficial principal obligations is perhaps the main reason for the existence (and expansion) of security device law (though one might reasonably criticize modern security device law for the method or extent to which it seeks to accomplish this goal).

To understand fully why security devices exist and the function they serve, we have to understand the limited remedies available to an "unsecured" creditor; that is, a creditor who does not have a "security device" backing up its debtor's principal obligation. Suppose Bank agrees to lend $10,000 to Borrower for the purchase of a used car. When the time comes to repay this loan, Borrower fails to do so; that is, she "defaults." What are Bank's options at this point? Obviously, Bank should try to seek some informal compromise arrangement with Borrower to avoid the expense of a legal battle. Failing that, though, in Louisiana as in most other places, enforcing an obligation through "normal" channels is a long and expensive process that often fails to produce a recovery of value for the creditor. Unsecured creditors like Bank face at least three main impediments to recovering value from a defaulting obligor.

First, an unsecured creditor can take little or no direct action against a recalcitrant debtor; rather, the creditor must engage the judicial system to enforce a defaulted obligation against the debtor's property. Since the mid-1800s, debtor's prison is no longer an option to coerce payment from defaulting debtors (though child support debtors sometimes are jailed for contempt of court for failure to pay their court-ordered support obligations). Creditors are limited to seeking recovery from the debtor's property, and only after obtaining a judgment and enforcing it through official channels. Creditors cannot engage in "self help" to take matters into their own hands. In our example, Bank cannot have Borrower jailed for refusal to fulfill her repayment obligation, and it cannot legally seize the car, even though Bank lent Borrower the very money used to purchase the car. Bank must file a lawsuit on the unpaid obligation, obtain a judgment, and send out the sheriff to find and seize Borrower's property (including, perhaps, the car).

Of course, the process of suing on a defaulted obligation is not free, even if the debtor fails to contest liability. Retaining an attorney to file the proper paperwork and have it served on the debtor by the sheriff often entails significant time and expense. Even after the creditor reduces the obligation to a judgment, that judgment must be enforced through a writ of garnishment (directing the debtor's bank or employer to turn over money in the debtor's bank account or unpaid wages) or a writ of "fieri facias" (often called a "fifa" writ, directing the sheriff to find, seize, and sell property belonging to the debtor and turn over the proceeds to the creditor). By the time the court process concludes and the sheriff arrives with a writ, the debtor may have no property of any value, or other creditors might have already taken what little valuable property the debtor had. So even if Bank goes through the process of obtaining a judgment (even a default judgment) against Borrower, by the time the sheriff arrives to seize, for example, the car that Borrower bought with Bank's money, the car might be damaged, destroyed, or missing, entailing at least further expense if not a total loss for Bank. And note that Bank's losses now include the wasted expense of its lawyer's fees, court costs, and the sheriff's fees.

Second, even if the debtor has valuable property, Louisiana law shields certain property from seizure in enforcement of a judgment. Such "exemption" statutes are part of the law of most states, and Louisiana's list of exempt property is moderately generous to debtors. Some of the most valuable property that an individual might own is protected from seizure in Louisiana, such as one car per household (up to $7,500 in value), household furniture, tools of the debtor's trade or profession, and up to $25,000 in equity value in residential property. La. Rev. Stat. 13:3881, 20:1. Corporations and other non-natural business entities do not enjoy these exemptions, but a sole proprietor, for example, might shield much of her valuable property even from business creditors. Back to our example, even if Bank obtains a judgment, and even though Bank lent Borrower the very money used to purchase the car, if it is Borrower's only car, the first $7,500 of value in that car is protected and reserved for Borrower (and if the car is worth $7,500 or less, the entire car is protected). The rest of Borrower's property may well also be shielded from Bank's legal advances, leaving Bank with no ready source of recovery.

Third, if the debtor commences a bankruptcy case before the sheriff seizes the debtor's property, all of the creditor's enforcement efforts might have been for naught. The creditor will stand in line with all of the other "general unsecured creditors," generally to receive perhaps 0%-10% of the creditor's claim. For individuals in Louisiana, the same exemptions laws apply both in and outside of bankruptcy, so Bank might recover no value from the car or any other property of Borrower, but at the very least, it will have to share whatever value is available with Borrower's other creditors. Avoiding the ill effects of the debtor's potential bankruptcy filing is perhaps the primary motivation for creditors' seeking one or more security devices.

Having a security device can allow the creditor to avoid all three of these impediments. As we shall see, some contractual security devices in identified items of property allow the creditor to avoid most or all of the judicial process and proceed directly to seizure of the property covered by the security device. In many cases, no ordinary judgment is necessary, and sometimes the intervention of the sheriff is not even required. Under limited circumstances, the creditor can engage in "self help," seizing the debtor's property immediately after default for a quick and reliable source of value. If Bank has a security interest in Borrower's car, Bank might well be able simply to send out its own "repo agent," grab Borrower's car, and sell the car at a private or public sale on Bank's own terms. Even if self help is not allowed, the process of enforcing many security devices is much quicker and easier than the ordinary judicial process. Given the decisive action authorized by some security device laws, the debtor has less time to damage, destroy, or spirit away the property. Moreover, if the creditor follows the rules discussed below, it can achieve first priority to take the debtor's property even after other creditors have already intervened.

Moreover, both exemptions law and bankruptcy law explicitly bow to the rights of creditors with properly arranged security devices. By their very terms, the exemptions laws do not shield property in which the debtor has voluntarily granted a security device by contract, La. Rev. Stat. 13:3881(B)(2), 20:1(C)(7), and secured creditors' rights are largely unaffected by the debtor's bankruptcy filing, particularly after a series of recent revisions to the federal Bankruptcy Code greatly enhanced the rights of secured creditors.

The law of security devices is thus largely about savvy contract creditors enhancing their rights in advance, before trouble arises, but this is not the whole story. Some security devices arise as a matter of law, and the intersection between consensual and nonconsensual interests is one of the most confusing elements of this area of the law. This book will discuss the four types of security devices available under the law of Louisiana and most other states, as well as where and how these security devices overlap and which takes precedence in the event of a conflict in the same property. The four types of security devices are as follows:

(1) consensual (contractual) security devices in the debtor's movable property ("security interests," governed by Article 9 of the Uniform Commercial Code, as adopted as Chapter 9 of Title 10 of the Louisiana Revised Statutes);

(2) consensual (contractual) and non-consensual security devices in the debtor's immovable property and immovable-property-related rights ("mortgages," governed by the Civil Code and several Code Ancillaries in Title 9 of the Louisiana Revised Statutes);

(3) nonconsensual interests arising as a matter of law in the debtor's movable and immovable property (technically called in Louisiana "privileges," but quite commonly referred to by the generic term "liens" — pronounced "leenz" — governed by the Civil Code and Revised Statutes); and

(4) agreements by third parties (called "sureties" or "guarantors") to pay the debtor's obligation(s) if the debtor does not ("suretyship," a nominate contract governed by the Civil Code).

Because lenders want maximum security, many of these devices occur together in common transactions. In part for this reason, this book brings all of the security devices together and analyzes their intersection and overlap, as well.

Louisiana Security Devices

Chapter 1

"UCC Article 9" and Security Interests in Movable Property

§1 Introduction, Categories of Movable Collateral

(a) Introduction

While it would be pointless to try to identify the "most important" or "most common" security device, we will begin with a security device that might arguably fit into either category. In pre-modern society, when land and interests in land represented the most valuable property, security devices in land and land-related interests (mortgage) were likely the most important, if not the most numerous. Today, with the advent of modern manufacturing and retailing operations and such common value-centers as cars and other heavy machinery, stocks and bonds issued by modern mega-corporations, and intellectual property rights, security devices in such "movables" are both extremely common and extremely valuable. Such "security interests" are also arguably the most complicated security devices, in part because movables cross state lines, change form, and sometimes produce or are exchanged for other movables. The law addresses these and other complex issues in sometimes confusing ways. Some of the most difficult questions of security devices law arise with respect to movable security, and such questions are perennial favorites on bar exams in Louisiana and elsewhere. This book is designed to present these issues in a straightforward way and to explain their resolution clearly, to make this difficult material accessible to everyone.

As noted in the introduction, the basic idea of this first security device is that the debtor grants the creditor a contingent property interest—called a "security interest"—in identified movable property—called the "collateral"—such that, if the obligor fails to perform the principal obligation, the creditor may seize the collateral from the debtor and seek reimbursement from the proceeds of its sale or other disposition. For example, if you borrow money from the bank to buy a car, the bank will likely require you to grant it a security interest in the car to secure your promise to repay the car loan. You own the car, but if you fail to fulfill any of the terms of the loan, the bank can seize your car, have it sold, and apply the sale proceeds to your outstanding indebtedness. Secured transactions involving movables can be much more complicated than this, but this common example illustrates the basic idea.

Contractual security interests in movables are subject to mostly the same rules in Louisiana and every other U.S. state. Fifteen years ago, Louisiana joined the rest of the nation in adopting all but the sales and leases provisions of the Uniform Commercial Code. "Article 9" of that Code comprises the provisions on "security interests" in movable property (sometimes called "personal property"), and Louisiana joined every other state in adopting the 2001 substantial revision of Article 9, which will be the focus of this chapter. Given the structure of Louisiana's statutory compilation, "Article 9" was codified as "Chapter 9" of title 10 of the Revised Statutes, although most Louisiana lawyers still refer to this law as "Article 9." The section numbering was kept intact, however, allowing for easy comparison with other states' law. For ease of reference, this chapter will refer to provisions of Louisiana's version of Article 9 by the common designation "§9-XXX." Although this law is generally the same as that adopted in all of the states, Louisiana lawmakers have made numerous small and not-so-small alterations to this "uniform" code, especially in Article 9. This book will point out and emphasize these differences as they arise.

(b) Categories of Article 9 Collateral

Security interests in movables represent an extremely valuable security device in part because of the range of property and property rights that they can encompass. Article 9 has its own system of categorizing various types of movable property, and lawyers in Louisiana and elsewhere commonly use these terms in everyday practice. Because security interests arise by contract, the intent of the parties determines exactly which property is covered, but sophisticated commercial parties generally use the terms developed in Article 9 to be sure to achieve the clearest and most comprehensive coverage possible (often explicitly incorporating the Article 9 definitions into their contracts).

The world of movable things can be divided into corporeal and incorporeal movables (or, if you prefer, tangible and intangible things). Some things seem to straddle the line between these two groups, generally because they have physical form, but their value derives not from the physical item, but from the fact that the item evidences certain incorporeal rights (e.g., promissory notes and stock certificates). Article 9 uses a variety of specific terms to identify the various types of collateral in these groups, and one should become familiar with some of the main terms to function comfortably in the world of movable financing.

(1) Corporeal Movables ("Goods")

Things that are valuable on their own (not for a separate right that they allow the possessor to exercise) are called "goods" in Article 9. §9-102(a)(44). "Goods" fall into one of four subgroups based on their use or intended use. These four categories are mutually exclusive; that is, a good can fall into only *one* of these groups:

(A) "Consumer Goods"

First, the law provides special protections to consumers who enter into secured transactions, so any goods that are "used or bought for use primarily for personal, family, or household purposes" (as opposed to business or commercial purposes) are called "consumer goods." §9-102(a)(23). It is extremely important to identify collateral that might be a "consumer good," as transactions involving such collateral are often subject to very different rules, as we shall see.

(B) "Farm Products"

Second, like consumers, farmers also enjoy special treatment under Article 9 and other laws. Thus, "farm products" constitute a second category of collateral, encompassing unprocessed agricultural "goods" owned by someone engaged in farming operations (defined in §9-102(a)(35)). This category includes crops (excluding standing timber, which has its own rules), livestock, supplies used in farming (e.g., manure, fertilizer, herbicides, etc.) and all other imaginable products of farming operations in their *unmanufactured* state. §9-102(a)(34). A thin and fuzzy line separates *unmanufactured* farm products from products that have undergone a manufacturing process and become business goods for sale (e.g., cheese), but we will not dwell on that distinction here. We will return to the special regime applicable to farm products, especially crops, later.

(C) "Inventory" and "Equipment"

The third and fourth subcategories encompass every other tangible good used for business purposes (including the business of farming). Goods held for sale or lease (including manufactured agricultural goods, like cheese) are "inventory." §9-102(a)(48). Raw materials and other non-farm supplies that will be used up in the course of conducting business are also "inventory" (e.g., cleaning supplies, heating oil, lubricant, etc.). Any good that does not fall into one of these other three categories is "equipment." §9-102(a)(33). Not only things like farm tractors, bulldozers, cash registers, computers, and the like fall into this category, but also office furniture and decorations (curtains and wall hangings), the refrigerator in the staff lounge, books and periodicals, and other items that are not held for sale or lease.

(2) In-Between Collateral (Documentary Collateral)

An intermediate general group of collateral has a corporeal form, but the value of the thing lies not in the "corpus," but in the right(s) that the thing allows the holder to exercise. For example, we all might agree that a share of a large corporation's stock has significant value, and we can touch the share certificate (although more on this below), but the value derives not from the paper on which the certificate is printed. The value lies in the property and governance rights with respect to the corporation that the stock certificate evidences. Such items that might be described loosely as "documentary" collateral are quite common, and they often represent some of the most valuable movables in society. Four common examples of categories of such collateral are as follows:

(A) "Instruments"

Checks and promissory notes (payable to the debtor) that qualify as "negotiable instruments" under Article 3 of the UCC are "instruments" that can serve as security under Article 9. §9-102(a)(47). Some other types of "commercial paper" that don't meet the negotiability requirements might be instruments, but checks (orders to a bank to pay the payee later) and notes (promises by the maker to pay the payee later) are the overwhelmingly most common type of this collateral.

(B) "Chattel Paper"

This often confusing concept simply describes a combination of two important rights, usually but not always memorialized in a piece of paper (although, more and more, recorded only electronically). Chattel paper is any "record" (including an electronic record, §9-102(a)(69)) that evidences both (1) a payment obligation, and (2) a security interest or lease in some "good." The easiest way to understand chattel paper is by remembering what are probably the two most common examples, both common among debtors who are car dealers: First, a retail installment sales agreement (RISA) evidences two important rights of the seller—a payment obligation of the buyer, to be collected in installments (the purchase price of, say, a car), and a security interest in the car to secure the buyer's payment of the installments. Car dealers often finance their inventory by giving security to a bank in their right to collect payments owed to them by customers. They often do this by granting an interest in all of their "chattel paper," which includes their own secured right to collect payment from car buyers. This is better than simply offering an interest in the buyers' installments ("accounts"), as the second right—the security interest—makes the account more secure and therefore more valuable. Second, any lease of movable property evidences two rights of value to the holder—the right to collect a payment obligation (the periodic rental payment) and the reversionary right in the leased property upon expiration of the lease term. Because a lease of movables evidences both of these rights together, the lessor can give a security interest in both rights together by offering the entire lease as security. Many car dealers also lease their cars, so offering the bank an interest in "chattel paper" encompasses the resulting rights whether the dealers sell the cars on secured credit or lease them to customers.

(C) "Documents"

This is not a generic term describing all papers in the filing cabinet, but a specific commercial term of art. "Documents" are documents of title regulated by Article 7 of the UCC. §9-102(a)(30). Common examples include warehouse receipts, bills of lading, and airbills. These are documents that acknowledge that someone else (e.g., the warehouse operator or a shipper) has merchandise that belongs to the holder of the document. The warehouse operator will release the merchandise (e.g., stored bales of cotton) only to someone who presents the warehouse receipt for the stored merchandise. Likewise for a shipper. These "documents" exclusively evidence the ownership rights in the property in storage or in transit, and they are thus just as valuable as the property itself.

(D) "Investment Property"

This term encompasses "securities" and "commodity contracts" of the kind traded in investment markets and regulated in part by Article 8 of the UCC. §9-102(a)(49). Stocks and bonds represent common examples, but brokerage accounts with brokers (like Charles Schwab) in which such investments are collected are also "investment property." Many of the most valuable stocks and bonds today are not evidenced by any piece of paper, and the rules for stocks, bonds, commodity contracts, and brokerage accounts in which such items are held differ depending upon whether the investments at issue are "certificated" or "uncertificated" and whether or not they are held "directly" by the investor or as part of the system of "indirect" holdings through broker-dealers. Investment property and the indirect holding system are discussed in greater detail below. *See below* §4(c)(3).

(3) *Incorporeal Movables*

A final general group of collateral includes movables that have no physical form. These "things" are pure rights, with no physical embodiment other than, perhaps, an informal paper record of the existence and scope of the right. Although one cannot touch these items, they often represent extremely valuable collateral that offers substantial security. Article 9 includes several categories of such intangible "rights-type" collateral, and four of the most common categories are as follows:

(A) *"Accounts"*

Any time someone promises to pay later for goods sold, leased, licensed or otherwise disposed of, or services rendered (or for a variety of other specific delayed-payment arrangements, like credit card balances or insurance premiums due), and the promise is not memorialized in a promissory note ("instrument," see above), the right of the seller/lessor to collect on that promise to pay is an "account." §9-102(a)(2). Manufacturers and merchants, for example, often borrow money and offer to creditors the right to collect on their customers' outstanding "accounts" (often called "accounts receivable" or "accounts payable") as collateral for loans. Be very careful to distinguish this type of account from the more specific "deposit account," which is an entirely separate and distinct category of collateral.

(B) *"Deposit Accounts"*

Like a general "account," a *deposit* account is a specific promise to pay money at a later date, but the promisor is always a depositary financial institution. "Deposit accounts" are checking, savings, and similar accounts maintained with entities engaged in banking (e.g., banks, credit unions, trust companies). §9-102(a)(29). Outside Louisiana, Article 9 governs security interests only in *commercial* deposit accounts, but Louisiana eliminated this restriction and subjected both consumer and business bank accounts to Article 9. (*See* §9-109(d)(13), which is "[reserved]"—that is, not adopted—in Louisiana's law).

(C) "General Intangibles"

All other property (except tort claims, see below) not categorized under other law as "immovable" (*see below* §3(d)) and not specifically categorized in Article 9 falls into the catch-all category of "general intangibles." §9-102(a)(42). Common examples of property that falls into this category include the following:

- rights in intellectual property (copyrights, trademarks, patents, etc.);
- "goodwill" (the reputational value of the right to do business using a certain name; e.g., the name "McDonald" has significant "goodwill" associated with it among members of the fast food-eating public, and the right to sell food under this name has significant value);
- "things in action," otherwise known as "choses in action," that encompass the right to sue on non-delictual causes of action (usually, conventional obligations);
- the right of the franchisee to operate under a franchise agreement.

(D) Tort Claims and Judgments

The potential recovery by the victim of a tort (in other words, the obligee's right to enforce a delictual obligation) represents potential value that can be used as collateral for a loan. A judgment represents a judicially confirmed or established right to collect on any obligation, conventional or delictual. Outside Louisiana, these two types of collateral are either restricted or limited. Louisiana law has "reserved" both the defining and limiting provisions of the uniform Article 9, so tort claims belonging to both consumers and businesses, as well as all judgments, can be offered as collateral security, and such transactions are governed by Article 9 in Louisiana. §§9-102(a)(13), 9-109(d)(9) and (12) and official comments. Technically, judgments fall within the category of "general intangibles," and tort claims make up a distinct but undefined category of collateral. Practically, however, the categorization of these types of collateral is of little importance, as security interests in tort claims and judgments must be described more specifically than by using the general category name to be valid in Louisiana. *See below* §2(c)(2).

§2 "Attachment" of Security Interests — The Security Agreement

A security interest is a way for savvy creditors to *contract* for the advantages of having priority reserved rights in movable collateral, so discussion of this law begins with the requirements of the contract, called a "security agreement." A security interest is enforceable against the debtor and "attaches" to the property serving as collateral only when the last of the three requirements in §9-203(b) has been met.

(a) Value

First, the law requires simply that "value has been given." This value is the obligation secured by the security interest, and recall that a security interest cannot exist without a principal obligation to secure. Generally, the value is given by the creditor to the debtor, but the value can be given to some other party, with the debtor offering to secure return of that value with the debtor's property. For example, a parent-debtor can grant a security interest in the parent's property to secure the obligation of a child-obligee to repay a loan. Article 9 is concerned only with the "debtor" as the holder of rights in the collateral, §9-102(a)(28), so the debtor need not be (although usually is) also the obligee of the secured obligation.

The "value" is most often a loan or series of loans made by the creditor to the debtor, but the term "value" is defined quite broadly in Article 1 of the UCC. (As of this writing, the definition is in section 1-201(44), although Article 1 is in the process of revision, and a very similar definition of value will likely appear in section 1-204 when the revision is adopted.) Any transfer of value qualifies, present or past, even a transfer that occurred in the distant past. The only hitch here is that "value" includes a promise to give value in the future *only* if the promise is a "binding commitment." If the recipient of the value can sue to recover the value if the creditor refuses to advance it, this commitment is "value" when the commitment is made. If, as is more often the case, the creditor reserves the right to refuse to advance the value later for any reason, this is not a binding commitment, and "value [will have] been given" only when the creditor actually grants the request and advances the loan. For example, banks often agree to extend a "line of credit" to borrowers, allowing a quicker and simplified application process for future loans. These lines of credit are not generally "binding commitments" (and do not therefore constitute "value" until a loan is actually made), as banks generally reserve the right to terminate the line and refuse to advance funds at any time and for virtually any reason.

(b) Rights in Collateral

As the Latin maxim goes, *"nemo dat quod non habet."* That is, no one can give what she does not have. In other words, to grant a valid security interest in a property right, the debtor must have the legal power to alienate that right. The transfer might be wrongful, as when a debtor-lessee purports to transfer an absolute ownership interest in the leased property, but the law must give the debtor the *power* to transfer the right at issue, leaving a potential struggle between secured creditor and owner. This requirement generally raises issues only with respect to future collateral. As we shall see below, debtors can grant security interests in property in which they do not yet have rights (e.g., property they might acquire in the future). A present security interest attaches to future property only when the debtor actually acquires rights in that property. Attachment is thus not retroactive to the time of execution of the security agreement (which is important to the question of priority of battling interests in property, although priority of a security interest is not always measured in terms of when it attaches to the collateral, as explained below, see §8).

(c) Security Agreement

Finally, security interests are consensual, so the debtor must have agreed to grant the security interest in identified property. The form or evidentiary requirements for this agreement differ depending upon the type of arrangement. Here we must draw a distinction between "possessory" and "non-possessory" security interests.

(1) Possessory Security Interests ("Pledge" and "Control")

In a "possessory" security interest, the creditor takes and keeps possession of the collateral. This sort of transaction was formerly governed by the "Pledge" articles of the Civil Code, and possessory security interests are often still called by this term today, as the debtor "pledges" the collateral physically to the creditor as security for an obligation, such as a loan from a pawn shop. Pledges are relatively rare today—at least the sort of pledges that occupy lawyers' time. Most debtors want or need to retain possession of the collateral, perhaps to use in producing value to fulfill the secured obligation. Nevertheless, if the security interest is "possessory," the final requirement for attachment is simply that the creditor take and retain possession of the collateral pursuant to the debtor's agreement (which can be oral, but of course should be in writing in most cases for evidentiary purposes). §9-203(b)(3)(B).

Some collateral cannot be "possessed," yet Article 9 sets up a separate mechanism for establishing a sort of "legal possession" that can serve the same function as physical possession. As will be discussed below (see §4(c)) some "rights-related" collateral is subject to the legal concept of "control," such as investment property, life insurance policies, and deposit accounts. If such collateral is under the creditor's "control," as defined below, then the debtor's oral agreement to grant a security interest in such collateral suffices for attachment (no need for a written agreement, although again, a written agreement is clearly preferable for evidentiary purposes). §9-203(b)(3)(C)–(D).

(2) Non-Possessory Security Interests ("Authenticated" Security Agreement)

Most debtors want or need to remain in possession of their collateral, and most creditors do not want to deal with the inconvenience of holding and preserving the collateral themselves. Therefore, the most common form of security interest today is non-possessory, and such security interests require a memorialized agreement to show that the creditor, who is not in possession of the collateral, nonetheless has rights in it. For most security interests, then, the third requirement for attachment is that "the debtor has authenticated a security agreement that provides a description of the collateral." §9-203(b)(3)(A).

Generally, the debtor "authenticates" a security agreement by signing a written document granting a security interest in the collateral. Such a document could be written on the back of a napkin: "I, Jason Kilborn, hereby grant a security interest in my 2000 Toyota Camry to Bank of America to secure a $10,000 loan advanced by the bank to me. /s/ Jason Kilborn." Many commercial security agreements in the United States, however, contain scores of pages and provide for a myriad of duties, protections, and events of default, among other provisions.

Article 9 defines "authenticate" broadly enough, however, to accommodate modern-age electronic commerce. Although the debtor can "authenticate" the agreement by signing it in pen and ink, the debtor can also "adopt a symbol" or "encrypt or similarly process a record" with the intention of identifying the debtor and accepting the document. §9-102(a)(7). A "record" is any medium of preserved information that is "retrievable in perceivable form." §9-109(a)(69). Thus, the debtor might "authenticate" a security agreement by sending the text of the agreement in an electronic mail message or even perhaps by leaving a message with the text of the agreement on a telephone answering machine system. The possibilities are not boundless, but they are quite broad.

The description of the collateral can be specific and detailed, although it generally need not be, and it often is quite general and broadly encompassing. The description must simply "reasonably identify" the collateral. §9-108(a). Specific descriptions of collateral by serial number or the like are certainly adequate, though one may, and most generally do, describe the collateral using the broad categories of Article 9 collateral discussed above ("inventory," "equipment," "accounts," "general intangibles."). In consumer transactions, however, "consumer goods" and the sub-categories of investment property are not adequate descriptions (more specific identification is required), and tort claims, life insurance policies, judgments, and a few other specific items of collateral must be described with greater specificity. §9-108(e). The only thing to avoid in any case is describing the collateral as "all assets" or "all of the debtor's property." Such "super-generic" descriptions are always insufficient. §9-108(c). Basic contract interpretation rules govern any eventual dispute regarding the scope of collateral covered. Accordingly, if Article 9 category descriptions are used, the agreement should make clear that both parties intend for the Article 9 definitions to govern, as the intent of the parties (not Article 9 or the dictionary) controls the meaning of terms used in the agreement.

The description of collateral can and often does include collateral not yet owned by the debtor. So-called "after-acquired collateral clauses" are quite common in commercial financing. Most commercial security agreements grant interests in the debtor's "presently owned and after-acquired" categories of collateral, or language of similar import. Article 9 specifically allows this. §9-204(a). In consumers transactions, after-acquired-collateral clauses apply only to consumer goods acquired within 10 days after the secured value has been given. §9-204(b)(1). Moreover, tort claims, judgments, life insurance policies, and other types of collateral that must be described specifically are practically and legally not subject to an after-acquired collateral clause. §9-204(b)(2)–(7). Similarly, security agreements can and often do secure value to be given in the future. §9-204(c). Thus, many security agreements include very broad "dragnet clauses" that provide for security interests in "all of Debtor's present and after-acquired [description of collateral] to secure any and all indebtedness owing from Debtor to Creditor now or at any point in the future."

§3 "Perfection" of Security Interests by Filing—the Financing Statement ("UCC-1")

It is often not enough simply to ensure that a security interest has attached to collateral and is enforceable against the debtor. A debtor can grant rights (including other security interests) in the same collateral to several creditors (intentionally or unintentionally), and some creditors get liens without the debtor's consent or even knowledge (e.g., after seizure by the sheriff). For each piece of collateral, the law lines up creditor claims in first, second, third, etc., order—defining who gets paid the proceeds from the sale of that collateral in what rank/priority order. When the proceeds run out after higher ranking creditors' secured claims have been paid, lower ranking creditors take nothing. If one secured creditor's secured claim has priority over another in certain collateral, that creditor's claim and its lien are called "senior," and the other creditor's claim and its lien are called "junior" or "subordinate." *Note well:* We are talking about priority of rights in *collateral* of particular *secured claims* here—not the priority in full payment of any creditor. The question is not which creditor will get paid first, but which *claim* will receive the reserved proceeds of *particular collateral* first. A creditor might have many claims against the debtor, some senior and some junior, some secured by collateral and some not.

Consensual secured creditors make their security interests effective against third parties (and establish the priority of their claims in the collateral) by "perfecting" their security interests. Perfection can occur only when the three steps for attachment (described above) have occurred *and* the requirements for perfection are met. §9-308(a). Usually, the perfection requirement is filing a "financing statement" on a form called a "UCC-1" in the state UCC records. Interests in some kinds of collateral can or must be perfected other than by filing, as the next section discusses. This section addresses filing a financing statement, the most common means of perfection.

While the security agreement establishes rights, the financing statement simply provides record notice. Accordingly, after 2001, the law no longer requires the debtor's signature on the financing statement. The filing must simply be "authorized" in an "authenticated record" by the debtor. §9-509(a). Recall from the discussion of authenticated security agreements above that an "authenticated record" is usually a signed writing, but it might be an electronic record transmitted or otherwise adopted by the debtor. The debtor rarely will authenticate a separate record to authorize a UCC-1 filing, however, although this might happen, for example, if the filing will occur during the negotiations before a security agreement is signed (a common tactic to enhance the creditor's priority position later). Instead, in most cases, the debtor's authentication of the security agreement acts as authenticated authorization to file a financing statement covering the collateral described in the security agreement (as well as any proceeds of that collateral, as discussed below). §9-509(b). The creditor can thus act unilaterally and quickly to preserve its rights in the collateral against third parties.

Rather than filing financing statements in the Secretary of State's office, as in most other states, creditors in Louisiana must file their UCC-1 forms in the UCC records of any parish clerk of court's office. §9-501(a). The parish clerks then transmit the filings to a centralized computer database maintained by the Secretary of State to enable searchers to find these filings. A UCC-1 filing theoretically gives third parties record notice that the debtor has already (or at least might have) given prior rights in certain collateral to the secured creditor, so any other future parties in interest should lend or engage in other dealings with respect to the collateral at their own risk.

The simple form UCC-1 asks for only a few pieces of information. The Louisiana form is available online from the Secretary of State's website at <http://www.sos.louisiana.gov/Portals/0/UCC-1.pdf>. For a filed financing statement to be "sufficient" (that is, effective), it must provide *at least* the names of the debtor and secured party along with a description of the collateral. §9-502(a).

(a) Indexing and Searching on the Debtor's Name

The single most important piece of information on a financing statement is the debtor's name, because that is the information used to place the form in the index and enable searching by others. The purpose of filing the UCC-1 is to put third parties on notice of the creditor's potentially adverse interest in the debtor's collateral; therefore, the law is quite strict about ensuring that the indexing information—the debtor's name—is property listed so third parties can locate the filing. A financing statement that lists the debtor's name incorrectly or inaccurately might well be ineffective.

Individuals might go by several names, including nicknames, and businesses often use trade names instead of their formal legal names. The form calls for the debtor's "exact full legal name," suggesting that nicknames and trade names should be avoided. For individuals, the law requires somewhat ambiguously that the statement list the debtor's "individual name," §9-503(a)(4), which might be interpreted to allow for a nickname if that is the name by which most people know the debtor. Courts in other states have generally rejected this approach, however, and good practice in any event calls for using the debtor's full legal name as listed on a birth certificate or Social Security card. For business entities, usually the full legal name listed on the organizational documents of the business is required. Most business debtors will be "registered organizations"; that is, organizations for which a state must maintain a public record of their existence. §9-102(a)(70). For example, corporations, limited partnerships (partnerships in commendam), and limited liability partnerships and companies (LLPs and LLCs) are "registered organizations." For such organizations, the debtor's name is *the* official name listed on the public record of the entity's existence (the articles of incorporation or organization, for example). §9-503(a)(1). Any name that differs from this full, official legal name is a "trade name," and the law is clear that trade names are neither necessary nor sufficient on a UCC-1. §9-503(b)–(c). For business associations that are not "registered organizations" (e.g., general partnerships), the proper name to use is the debtor's "organizational" name. §9-503(a)(4). Presumably this means using the name in the partnership agreement, or perhaps even using all of the partners' names.

Slight misspellings might make it impossible for later searchers to find the financing statement in the records, or they might simply produce some momentary confusion. Which effect the error would produce in a search for the financing statement determines the effectiveness *vel non* of the UCC-1. The law sets up a practical test of how to deal with debtor names that are close but not quite right. If the financing statement lists the debtor's name substantially correctly, but with "minor errors or omissions," the financing statement is effective so long as it is not "seriously misleading." §9-506(a). With respect to the debtor's name, the "seriously misleading" test is subjective, based on each state's searching system. A statement with "minor errors or omissions" is nonetheless effective (i.e., not "seriously misleading") as a matter of law if a hypothetical search on the debtor's *correct* name using the state's search logic would find the slightly incorrect financing statement. §9-506(c). Thus, an error that would prevent the computer search from turning up the financing statement is ineffective to perfect a security interest, but if a search on the proper name would find the slightly erroneous financing statement (thanks to more liberal search logic), such an error is "*de minimis*" and has no effect on the effectiveness of the filed financing statement. The effect of minor spelling errors can thus change over time as the state implements different indexing and search logic systems.

(b) Description of Collateral

The description of collateral in the financing statement usually tracks the description in the security agreement. This is the best practice, and it is probably the most common practice. Debtors might authorize filings covering more collateral in anticipation of later transactions, however. Such a filing would not create rights in the more broadly described property, but it would enhance the creditor's position vis-à-vis third parties in advance if the debtor were to grant rights in other property later. In such cases, the law places virtually no restrictions on the collateral description in the financing statement. Here, "super-generic" descriptions such as "all of the debtor's property" or "all assets" are sufficient, although such a filing likely must be separately authorized in a separate authenticated record. §9-504.

(c) Other Information

The UCC-1 form calls for several other items of information that should be completed if the clerk is to accept the filing, such as the debtor's and secured creditor's addresses, the debtor's business form, organizing jurisdiction, and identification number. Errors in this information will likely have no effect on the effectiveness of a financing statement accepted for filing. *But see* §§9-338, 9-506(a) (addressing errors that, under the circumstances, produce real or perhaps even hypothetical potential for misleading searchers).

(d) Component Parts ("Fixtures") and Fixture Filings

Sometimes movable property is so closely related to an immovable (e.g., land or a building) that a conflict might arise between movable security law and the law governing immovable property (sometimes called "real estate"). This is true, for example, of oil, gas, and other minerals in the ground, as well as standing timber and unharvested crops, all of which will become valuable only after extraction or harvest. Similarly, some movable property becomes so affixed to immovable property (e.g., heating and air conditioning units, plumbing and electrical installations, etc.) that it is deemed to become part of the immovable (i.e., no longer movable at all), and an interest arises in such property under immovable property law. Technically, in Louisiana we call such a formerly movable thing a "component part" of the immovable. In Article 9, such things are called "fixtures," because they have become "affixed" to immovable property. §9-102(a)(41). Ordinary building materials that become "affixed" to an immovable are specifically excluded from Article 9, §9-334(a), but other movables remain potentially subject to Article 9 even after they become part of an immovable.

A fierce debate occurred recently surrounding the definition in Louisiana law of when a movable thing becomes so affixed to an immovable as to constitute a component part (or fixture). The debate resulted in an amendment to the Civil Code to clarify the broad meaning of the term "component part." Civ. C. art. 466. An extended discussion of this definition is beyond the scope of this book. If a creditor wants to take a security interest in a movable that *might* become a component part of an immovable, the creditor would be well advised to follow the special rules regulating "fixtures."

In addition to "fixtures," a few other specific types of collateral are governed by the special rules for land-related collateral. Some such interests are categorized or treated quite differently under Louisiana's version of Article 9 than under the law of other states.

(1) Unharvested Crops

Under Louisiana property law, crops still growing in the ground or attached to trees are "component parts" of the land if they are owned free and clear by the landowner. Civ. C. art. 463. But if the landowner has granted a security interest in the crops to a creditor (or if they are owned by someone other than the landowner), crops are not component parts, but rather "movables by anticipation." Civ. C. art. 474. Thus, crops subject to a security interest are not considered under the special "land-related" collateral rules. Instead, crops are subject to the normal Article 9 rules, supplemented by a specific regime for perfection of interests in farm products, which requires a special filing in the agricultural "central registry" of the state. *See below* § 16(c); § 9-311(a)(2); La. Rev. Stat. 3:3651 *et seq.*

(2) Standing Timber

In Louisiana, trees that are not destined for harvest are either separate and distinct immovables or component parts of the land on which they are growing, Civ. C. arts. 463–464, and such trees are not subject to Article 9 at all. Standing timber constitutes "goods" governed by Article 9 and other special state law rules only if it is "to be cut and removed" by someone other than the landowner, and only if it is subject to a "recorded timber conveyance." § 9-102(a)(44)(ii). The timber must have been conveyed to someone other than the landowner (either immediately, as standing timber, or for the future, as lumber immediately after future harvest) by a conveyance document executed by the record owner of the land and recorded in the proper parish conveyance records. § 9-109(d)(16). Note that "the debtor" in such case is the third person to whom the trees have been conveyed in advance, who will own the valuable lumber after harvest. If the landowner were to use her own standing timber as collateral, mortgage law would govern the transaction. Once the trees are cut down, of course, they become movable lumber, subject to the normal Article 9 rules, again supplemented by special agriculture-related filing rules. *See below* § 16(c).

(3) "As-Extracted Collateral"

Oil, gas, and other minerals in the ground are treated as immovable property, but like timber, oil and gas and other minerals will become movable (and their primary value will become available) when extracted from the ground. Article 9 carves out a category of collateral called "as-extracted collateral," which encompasses oil, gas, and minerals that are the objects of security interests that are contracted while the minerals are still in the ground but that attach only upon extraction of the minerals from the ground. §9-102(a)(6)(A). This interest can be granted by either the landowner or by a third person with a mineral right (specially defined in §9-102(d)(13)). In addition, in Louisiana, "as-extracted collateral" includes the "accounts" arising out of the sale at the wellhead or minehead of such minerals (as well as "royalties" paid to the landowner or mineral right holder based on production volume). §9-102(a)(6)(B). Oil, gas, or minerals might *also* qualify as "inventory" after extraction, and security interests contracted in oil, gas, and minerals *after* their extraction are not subject to any special rules. But for security interests contracted in advance of the minerals' being "reduced to possession," the special "land-related" rules apply to perfection of security interests in such "as-extracted collateral."

Louisiana's law governing perfection of security interests in as-extracted collateral and "fixtures" differs substantially from the law of other states. A creditor can perfect an Article 9 security interest in these "land-related" types of collateral *only* by making a "fixture filing" with respect to the collateral. §9-502(b). A fixture filing differs from a "normal" UCC-1 filing in Louisiana only in that a fixture filing must describe not only the collateral, but also the related immovable property (with the level of detail required to make a mortgage effective against third parties, see below §10(b)(4)). §9-502(b)(3). The box on the UCC-1 form indicating that it is a "fixture filing" must be checked, and the name of the record owner of the immovable must be indicated (if other than the debtor, as will definitely be the case, e.g., with standing timber). §9-502(b)(1), (4).

Fixture filings in Louisiana are made in the same place as "normal" UCC-1 filings—in the UCC records of any parish clerk of court's office, regardless of the location of the immovable property involved.

This is perhaps the single most significant non-uniformity in Louisiana's version of Article 9. Outside Louisiana, fixture filings are made in the land records (mortgage records) of the county where the immovable (real property) is.

With respect to "component parts" (fixtures), Louisiana law differs from the uniform Article 9 in three other important respects. First, outside Louisiana, creditors *can* perfect security interests in fixtures by making a normal, non-fixture filing with respect to the collateral. Such a filing is of limited value, but against certain creditors, such as the debtor's later trustee in bankruptcy, for example, a "normal" filing is sufficient outside Louisiana to protect the secured creditor's rights. This is not true in Louisiana. Security interests in fixtures can be perfected *only* by fixture filing in Louisiana. §9-334(a) and official comments.

Second, Louisiana law requires that the fixture filing be accomplished *before* the movable is affixed to the immovable. §§9-102(a)(40), 9-334(a). Once a movable becomes a fixture, it is regarded as falling within the exclusive domain of Louisiana immovable property law. A fixture filing is thus an absolute necessity to reserve an Article 9 interest in a good before it becomes a component part of an immovable. If a fixture filing is not made *before* the good is affixed to the immovable, not only is a security interest in that fixture not perfected, it does not "continue" in the fixture and is thus unenforceable, even against the debtor. §9-334(a).

Finally, consumer goods that become fixtures are excluded from Article 9 in Louisiana and cannot be subject to a continuing security interest at all. §9-334(a). Once a consumer good becomes a fixture, any security interest is stripped from the good. Only mortgage or other immovable property law governs consumer-good component parts (except for manufactured homes, which for reasons of space and focus, this book will not discuss).

§4 Alternative Perfection Methods

Filing a financing statement in the UCC records of any parish clerk of court's office is the default method for perfecting all security interests, §9-310(a), and it is sufficient in *almost* all cases. Security interests in certain types of collateral can be perfected in other ways, however, and some *must* be perfected in a different way. This section outlines the alternatives.

(a) Filing Outside the UCC System (Including Certificate of Title Collateral)

For some types of collateral, other special filing rules trump the general rule about filing in the state UCC system to perfect. The first group of such special filing rules are found in federal law. Under the Supremacy Clause of the U.S. Constitution, provisions of federal law trump any inconsistent provisions of state law (such as Article 9 of the UCC), but Article 9 specifically bows to any different perfection requirements under federal law. §9-311(a)(1). Two prominent examples of such laws affect perfection of security interests in intellectual property and aircraft. The Copyright Act arguably requires a filing in the Copyright Office in Washington, D.C., to perfect any interest (including a security interest) in a copyright, although this is not entirely clear. 11 U.S.C. §205. Perfection of security interests in patents and trademarks may also require filing in the Patent and Trademark Office (PTO) in Washington, D.C., although this is even less clear. It is relatively clear, on the other hand, that federal law requires a filing with the Federal Aviation Administration in Oklahoma City, OK, to perfect a security interest in an aircraft (or certain aircraft parts). 49 U.S.C. §1403.

State law contains the second group of statutes that provide for a different filing location, primarily for agricultural products and collateral covered by certificates of title (cars, trucks, and in some states boats). Article 9 specifically defers to these other laws and their requirements for filing perfection. §9-311(a)(2)–(3). The special rules on filing in the agricultural registry are discussed below in the section on crop privileges. *See below* §16(c). As for cars and other collateral covered by a certificate of title, in most states, other state law says that security interests in such collateral must be perfected by having the security interest noted officially on the title certificate. One usually submits to the Department of Motor Vehicles the original title certificate and an application asking that the lien be noted on it.

Louisiana law is uniquely different. Instead of noting their liens on the title certificates for (1) motor vehicles, (2) boats (technically called "vessels") worth more than $2,500 and first transferred on or after July 1, 2008, and (3) outboard motors first transferred on or after January 1, 2011, creditors in Louisiana may perfect security interests in such titled collateral only by filing a UCC-1 financing statement in a specific office. For motor vehicles, the filing is made in the office of motor vehicles, part of the Department of Public Safety and Corrections, while for boats and outboard motors, the correct filing office is the Department of Wildlife and Fisheries. §§ 9-311(b); 9-501(a)(1), (3). In addition, financing statements for such collateral must include more specific descriptions of the collateral than would generally be required. *See* § 9-504(3)-(5). For motor vehicles, the statement must provide the year of manufacture, make, model, body style, and vehicle identification number. For boats, the description must include the hull identification number, vessel length, model year or year built, name of manufacturer or model, vessel type, propulsion type, and principal material of hull construction. Outboard motors must be specifically described by serial number, year manufactured, and name of manufacturer or model. Generally, the secured creditor will also retain possession of the relevant title certificate until the secured debt is paid off, but this is not required for perfection; it is simply a practical strategy to prevent fraud by debtors.

This rule is subject to one very important exception. Dealers might grant a security interest in part or all or their inventory of new or used motor vehicles, boats, or outboard motors. The special rules for titled collateral do not apply to such items *held for sale or lease.* Security interests in such collateral can be perfected by ordinary UCC-system filing; *e.g.,* against the dealer's "inventory." §§ 9-311(d), 9-504(3)–(5).

In addition to these "other" filing systems, the UCC offers three other ways of perfecting certain security interests that do not involve filing at all. The availability (or requirement) of each depends upon the type of collateral and the specific transaction involved.

(b) Possession

For any type of collateral that has physical form (or at least a physical embodiment that the business world recognizes as exclusively defining an incorporeal right, like checks, promissory notes, and stock certificates), the secured creditor can perfect a security interest in such property simply by taking and holding possession of the collateral. §9-313. As discussed above, this type of "possessory" security interest was formerly governed by the Civil Code articles on "pledge" or "pawn," and such transactions concern lawyers relatively infrequently today. If the collateral is "money" (e.g., foreign currency reserves) or a collateral mortgage note (discussed in great detail below, see §13(c)), possession is the only possible means of perfection. §9-312(b)(3)–(4). For other types of corporeal collateral, possession is an alternative to filing, but possession is slightly better for "documentary"-type collateral, like instruments, for reasons of priority, discussed below, see §8(c)(2).

(c) "Control"

The 2001 revision of Article 9 introduced a new concept into the law of movable security: control. A special defined term of art, "control" is the functional equivalent of possession for certain types of incorporeal "rights-type" collateral. Control is an alternative or exclusive method of perfection (and attachment, as discussed above, see §2(c)(1)) only for a few identified types of collateral, §9-314(a), and how one establishes control differs depending upon the type of collateral at issue. This section will address only three of the most common types of collateral subject to "control": deposit accounts, life insurance policies, and investment property. Establishing control is the *only* method of perfecting a security interest in deposit accounts and life insurance policies, and control is a superior alternative to perfecting security interests in investment property. §§9-312(b), 9-314.

(1) Control Over Deposit Accounts

A creditor can perfect a security interest in a deposit account *only* by establishing control over that account in one of three ways set out in §9-104. First, if the secured creditor is the bank where the deposit account is maintained, it has control automatically. Second, if the creditor is not the depositary institution, it can get control through a so-called "control agreement" among the bank, the debtor, and the secured party. This agreement must be memorialized in an "authenticated record" (*see above* § 2(c)(2)) in which the parties agree that the bank can and will follow the secured creditor's instructions with respect to disposition of the money in the deposit account without further consent by the debtor. Finally, the secured creditor can also establish control if the creditor "becomes the bank's customer with respect to the deposit account," generally by having the secured creditor added as a "security joint account holder" with the debtor on the account. As an account holder, the secured creditor can direct the bank to do with the money on deposit whatever the creditor wishes, and the bank is obliged to follow its customer's instructions, just like in other joint account situations.

(2) Control Over Life Insurance Policies

Secured transactions in which a life insurance policy (and its potential proceeds) are used as collateral for a loan are not governed by Article 9 in most states. Louisiana law eliminated this exclusion in the uniform law, so Louisiana's Article 9 contains special provisions regarding life insurance policies as collateral. The security agreement must describe the life insurance policy collateral more specifically (e.g., by policy number), § 9-108(d)(3), and such security interests can be perfected *only* by establishing control over the policy in one of two ways set forth in § 9-107.1. First, if the secured creditor is the insurance company that issued the policy, the creditor automatically has control. Second, if the creditor is not the issuing insurance company, the creditor establishes control by having the insurance company "authenticate a record acknowledging notice of the granting of a security interest to the secured party in the policy." Generally, this will simply be a one-page document, signed by an authorized representative of the insurer, indicating that it has received notice that a security interest has been granted in the policy (though this notice need not—and should not be construed to—acknowledge that the security interest has *properly* attached to the policy). Certain other requirements might apply in addition if the beneficiary of the policy is not the insured (or the insured's estate). *See* § 9-107.1(b).

(3) Control Over Investment Property

Security interests in investment property (e.g., stocks, bonds, commodity contracts) may be perfected by filing, but perfection by control is superior. To understand the various ways of establishing control over investment property, one must understand the diverse ways in which investors hold securities today.

In the not-too-distant past, companies issued paper certificates representing every investor's stock and bond holdings. Generally, these certificates were in "registered" form; that is, the name of each holder was written on the certificate and recorded in the company's securities register (some other securities were issued in "bearer" form, with no indication of the exclusive owner's name on the face of the certificate). To trade these securities, investors would transfer the paper certificates, generally with endorsements (signatures on the back), much like people pass ("negotiate") checks today. The new owner of the stock shares or bond would then send the endorsed certificate to the company and request a new certificate in the new owner's name. This system worked fine—and still works quite well today—for companies with relatively low trading volume. Even today, smaller companies (even some publicly traded companies) continue to issue "certificated securities," and transactions concerning these securities continue to be accomplished by endorsing, trading, and re-registering paper certificates.

For larger companies whose securities enjoyed a more and more robust trading market, the expense, inconvenience, and delay of dealing with millions of these paper certificates ultimately proved unbearable. The investment industry sought to develop a new and more efficient system based on electronic records, rather than on bulky paper certificates. For reasons that lie far beyond the scope of this book, two different systems developed as a result of this desire to move away from individual paper certificates.

One segment of the industry developed a paperless system of "uncertificated securities." As the name suggests, these companies did away with paper certificates and registers altogether. Uncertificated securities are evidenced only by a notation in the companies' electronic register. These companies might well issue paper (or electronic) statements of holdings, but the securities themselves are me-morialized only in electronic records kept by the companies or their agents. Trading in uncertificated securities is accomplished by orders directed by investors to a company's registrar to alter the electronic books of the company to reflect new ownership of identified securi-ties. Relatively few companies undertook this aggressive new ap-proach to securities bookkeeping. The securities of mutual fund com-panies are often "uncertificated," but a different system has emerged (at least for now) as the more common method for moving away from reams of paper certificates.

The majority of the securities of the largest publicly traded com-panies in the United States today are memorialized by a certificate, but individual investors do not hold "certificated securities." Instead, most large company securities are held "indirectly" through accounts with broker-dealers and large investment banks, and individual in-vestors' holdings here again are evidenced only by electronic records of "securities accounts" maintained by these brokers and banks. In the "indirect" holding system, companies issue so-called "jumbo" certificates, representing millions or even billions of shares of stock (or dollars of a bond issue). The jumbo certificate is generally issued in the name of "Cede & Co.," the nominee name of a company called the Depository Trust Company (DTC). DTC is a special-purpose company organized by hundreds of investment banks and broker-dealers for the purpose of holding securities on behalf of the banks'/brokers' investing customers. Rather than trading paper cer-tificates every time a security is traded by their investing customers, these banks/brokers simply adjust their internal account records (for trades between customers of the same bank or broker-dealer) or the National Securities Clearing Corporation adjusts the banks'/brokers' accounts with DTC (for trades between customers of different banks and broker-dealers). Thus, DTC holds the securities "indirectly" for the ultimate investors and agrees to follow their instructions with re-spect to exercising the financial and governance rights that the secu-rities represent. Individual investors thus own not the securities themselves, but "securities entitlements"; that is, an entitlement to exercise the financial and governance rights that the securities rep-resent.

The system of certificated, uncertificated, and indirectly held securities entitlements and securities accounts is governed by Article 8 of the UCC. Article 9 defers to Article 8 in defining the steps necessary to establish control over the various types of investment property holdings. §9-106(a).

(A) Certificated Securities

One establishes control over securities with paper certificates by taking "delivery" (usually simple passage of possession, §8-301(a)) of the certificate and, if the certificate is in "registered" form (listing a specific named holder and requiring endorsement to transfer rights), by getting the certificate properly endorsed (to the named deliveree or in blank) or reregistered on the company's books in the name of the deliveree. §8-106(a)–(b). Note that the law refers to the deliveree here as a "purchaser," which includes secured creditors taking security interests. §1-201(32)–(33) under current Article 1, §1-201(b)(29)–(30) under the revised version. Thus, perfection by control in a certificated security in most cases requires the secured creditor to take possession of the certificate *and* have the debtor endorse the certificate over to the creditor (either specially or in blank). Simply taking possession is not sufficient for securities that are not in "bearer" form. §9-313(a).

(B) Uncertificated Securities

Since uncertificated securities have no corporeal form, establishing control or any other property interest over such securities requires the cooperation of the issuing company. A secured creditor can establish control over uncertificated securities in one of two ways. First, it can take "delivery" of an uncertificated security by having the issuing company register the creditor as the owner. §§8-106(c)(1), 8-301(b). Second, the secured creditor can obtain a "control agreement" from the issuer in which the issuer agrees that "it will comply with instructions originated by the [secured creditor] without further consent by the registered owner." §8-106(c)(2). Apparently, this agreement can be oral, as the law makes no reference to an "authenticated record," although good practice would call for a record.

(C) Indirect Holdings—Securities Entitlements and Securities Accounts

Rights to "securities entitlements" maintained through a broker in the indirect holdings system are quite similar to the rights to funds maintained by a bank in a deposit account. Therefore, one establishes control over indirectly held securities entitlements in much the same way as for a deposit account. First, if the creditor is the bank/broker maintaining the securities entitlement or account, that person automatically has control over the account and all entitlements in it. § 8-106(e). Second, if the secured creditor is not the bank/broker, it can get control through a "control agreement" in which the bank/broker agrees that it "will comply with entitlement orders originated by the [creditor] without further consent by the entitlement holder." § 8-106(d)(2). Here again, unlike for a deposit account control agreement, the agreement need not necessarily be in an "authenticated record," although this would be the best practice. Finally, the secured creditor can also establish control if the creditor "becomes the entitlement holder"; that is, if the creditor is added as a joint account holder on the securities account or is registered on the bank's/broker's books as the owner of the entitlements in the account. § 8-106(d)(1).

(d) Automatic Perfection—PMSIs in Consumer Goods

Some security interests are perfected the moment they attach to collateral, with no need to take any other action. Most of these are specific and relatively esoteric transactions that are not of general interest. *See* § 9-309(2)–(12). Only one such transaction is worth a comment here: Purchase-money security interests in consumer goods are automatically perfected upon attachment. § 9-309(1). We already know that a consumer good is any tangible thing used or bought for use primarily for personal, family, or household use. *See above* § 1(b)(1)(A); § 9-102(a)(23). Consumer goods are usually not hard to identify. A "purchase-money security interest" (often called a PMSI, either spelled out or pronounced "pim-zee") is a security interest that secures repayment of the obligation (a loan or credit sale) incurred and actually used to acquire the collateral. §9-103. A loan used for multiple purposes is a PMSI only to the extent that it was used to acquire the collateral subject to the security interest. Note that the debtor need not *intend* to grant a PMSI in collateral; a security interest is a PMSI if it satisfies the criteria, regardless of the parties' intent.

So for example, suppose Creditor lent Debtor $20,000, Debtor used $10,000 of that money to buy a personal pleasure boat and the other $10,000 to pay off some household expenses, and Debtor granted Creditor a security interest in the boat and some other household property to secure the entire $20,000 loan. The security interest in the household property is not a PMSI, because it does not secure repayment of any credit used to acquire the property. The security interest in the boat is a PMSI *to the extent* that it secures an obligation actually used to acquire the boat. §9-103(b)(1). Thus, the boat is subject to a $10,000 purchase-money security interest (since this much of the loan was used to acquire the boat), and *this* security interest was automatically perfected as soon as it attached to the boat. Pursuant to Debtor's agreement, the boat is *also* subject to a non-purchase-money security interest securing the other $10,000 of the loan, as that money was not actually used to acquire the boat. This security interest must be perfected separately (probably by filing). This dual security interest might not matter in the end, but this example illustrates that a security interest is a PMSI *to the extent* that it qualifies as one on the facts, although a non-PMSI might also attach to the collateral. If and only if the collateral is consumer goods, the PMSI is automatically perfected, but the non-PMSI must be perfected independently. Of course, PMSIs in non-consumer goods must be perfected independently in every case. One small caveat: this rule does not apply to collateral subject to non-UCC perfection rules, specifically cars and titled boats worth more than $2,500, in which security interests can be perfected *only* by filing with the OMV or Department of Wildlife and Fisheries, as discussed above in §4(a). §9-309(1).

§5 Attachment and Perfection of Security Interests in Proceeds

One particularly complicating aspect of movable security device law is that movables can be (and often are) exchanged for other movables, and they sometimes produce other movables. Unlike mortgage law, security interest law governs both the original collateral and almost anything received in exchange for or produced by the original collateral, and an entirely different and separate set of rules governs the "follow-on" movables. Indeed, Article 9 even has a separate definition for one subset of such follow-on collateral: proceeds. The simplest and perhaps most common example of "proceeds" is whatever the debtor takes in exchange for selling the collateral (e.g., a promise to pay, a check, money, other property, etc.). But "proceeds" is defined more broadly in Article 9 to encompass lots of other things the debtor might acquire as a result of having rights in the original collateral. "Proceeds" includes not only anything the debtor acquires upon the "sale, lease, license, or other disposition of collateral," but also anything "collected on or distributed on account of" the collateral, as well as any "rights arising out of" the collateral. §9-102(a)(64). The scope of property encompassed by this broad definition of "proceeds" is not altogether clear, but it certainly sweeps broadly.

From a practical standpoint, most sophisticated creditors draft their security agreements specifically to take a continuing security interest in any proceeds of their original collateral. To avoid any semantic haggling, they often take an interest in any "products, rents, profits, and offspring" of the collateral, as well. These terms might arguably not fall within the Article 9 definition of "proceeds," so careful creditors broaden and confirm their rights by contract.

(a) Automatic Attachment

But Article 9 is quite generous to creditors who forget to include such language in their security agreements. At least as to "proceeds," as defined in Article 9, §9-315(a)(2) provides that a security interest in collateral automatically attaches to any identifiable proceeds of that collateral as a matter of law. So even if the security agreement contains no such grant, the secured creditor gets an interest in the proceeds of collateral, theoretically as a substitute for the collateral that the debtor has just alienated in exchange for the proceeds. Note that the proceeds have to be "identifiable" as deriving from the original collateral. For proceeds like money, commingled with other non-proceeds money, the law might step in under certain circumstances to presume a tracing mechanism and identify which money is proceeds of collateral and which is not. It is good practice, however, to require the debtor to segregate collateral proceeds from other property so the creditor can trace the line between collateral and proceeds (and proceeds of proceeds, etc.).

But that's not all. In a move that I like to call the "2X effect," Article 9 also generally preserves the creditor's security interest in the collateral in the hands of the person who acquired it from the debtor. Unless the secured creditor authorizes the disposition of the collateral *free and clear of the security interest* (impliedly or expressly), a security interest follows the collateral into the hands of the recipient of the collateral. §9-315(a)(1). Note that the creditor might authorize the disposition of collateral yet not authorize disposition *free and clear* of the security interest. The law includes a choice few exceptions to this rule to protect people who acquire goods from debtors, *see below* §8(b), but the general rule is that, following disposition of collateral, the creditor has a security interest in *both* the original collateral in the recipient's hands *and* the proceeds of the collateral in the debtor's hands. The creditor's collateral doubles instantly. The recipient is not generally personally liable on the secured obligation, of course, but if the debtor defaults, the creditor might be able to come and take the original collateral from the unsuspecting recipient later on. For this reason, one of the primary "due diligence" tasks of lawyers representing buyers at closings on large asset sales is to make sure no secured creditor of the seller has a security interest in the thing to be acquired—or that the secured creditor has authorized the sale free and clear of the security interest (perhaps in exchange for direct payment of part or all of the purchase price).

(b) Automatic and Non-Automatic Perfection

While having an *attached* security interest is nice, the creditor would prefer to have a *perfected* security interest, and the law comes to the creditor's aid here, too, in one of the most complex provisions in Article 9. As for the original collateral in the recipient's hands, the original security interest was most likely perfected by filing, and the disposition will not affect this perfection in most cases (although see below §7(c)). The original UCC-1 financing statement naming the debtor remains effective to perfect the follow-on interest in the collateral now owned by someone with an entirely different name! §9-507(a)–(b). Unperfected security interests remain unperfected, of course, following disposition. The law only helps those who help themselves.

As for the proceeds, §9-315(c) and (d) provide a complex test for determining whether or not the new security interest is (and will remain) perfected. Again, if the interest in the original collateral was not perfected, the interest in the proceeds will not be perfected until the creditor takes the steps necessary to do so. If the interest in the original collateral was perfected (again, most likely by filing), the new security interest in the proceeds is automatically perfected for a 20-day "grace" period, and it continues perfected on the 21st day and thereafter if one of four sets of conditions is met. §9-315(c)–(d). Indeed, if one of these four sets of conditions is met, the proceeds security interest is deemed to have been perfected from the time of perfection of the original security interest, greatly enhancing the priority of the interest. §9-322(b)(1).

First, in any case, the security interest in the proceeds can be perfected pursuant to the original UCC-1 financing statement if the description of collateral in the original UCC-1 covers the proceeds (by category type or specific description, but not simply by mentioning that "proceeds" are covered). The effect of financing statements is not restricted to specific transactions, so they can perfect security interests totally unanticipated by the parties, including later-arising interests in proceeds (again, even if the security agreement did not provide for any interest in proceeds). For example, suppose Debtor authorized in a separate authenticated record the filing of a financing statement covering Debtor's "present and after-acquired equipment and inventory," but Debtor granted Creditor a security interest only it its inventory. If Debtor sells some inventory for cash and uses that cash to buy a piece of equipment, Creditor will have a security interest automatically as a matter of law in the equipment (as proceeds of proceeds of the original inventory collateral), and that interest will be perfected by the original UCC-1, which lists "equipment." This result follows even if Debtor and Creditor neither foresaw nor intended this.

Second, if the original financing statement does not describe the proceeds, the secured creditor can file an amendment to the original UCC-1 to describe the proceeds within the 20-day grace period (or perfect in some other way within the period). §9-315(d)(3). Note that the creditor needs no separate authorization to do this, as the debtor's authenticating a security agreement operates as automatic authorization to file not only the original UCC-1 describing the original collateral, but also authorization to file an amendment to add a description of new proceeds. §9-509(b)(2). In our example above, if the original financing statement only covered Debtor's "inventory," Creditor could perfect its interest in the new equipment-proceeds by filing an amended UCC-1 describing the inventory and the new equipment-proceeds (probably by specific description, as a general "all equipment" description would be overbroad). By the way, if the new UCC-1 is filed after the 20-day grace period expires, the new security interest in the equipment-proceeds will be perfected, but this will reset the creditor's priority date to the day of the filing of the new UCC-1 (rather than the original date of filing of the original UCC-1).

Third, if the proceeds are identifiable "cash proceeds," the security interest in the proceeds is automatically and continuously perfected. §9-315(d)(2). "Cash proceeds" are largely what one would suspect, including cash and checks, but also the deposit account into which such cash or checks were deposited (to the extent of the value of the proceeds money or checks). §9-102(a)(9). In our example, if Debtor sells inventory in an immediate exchange for cash or a check, Creditor has an automatically and continuously perfected security interest in the cash or check and in the extent of their value placed into Debtor's deposit account.

Finally, if the three-part test set forth in section 9-315(d)(1) is satisfied, the security interest in the proceeds will be automatically and continuously perfected as a matter of law. First, the original collateral must be covered by a filed financing statement. Second, the proceeds must be collateral in which a security interest can be perfected by filing in the same office where the original UCC-1 was filed (which excludes, most notably, cars that are not proceeds of other cars). Note that, unlike in our first set of conditions discussed above, the description of collateral in the original UCC-1 here need not cover the proceeds. Finally, the proceeds must not have been acquired with cash proceeds.

A couple of examples are crucial to understanding this odd three-part test. Recall our example in which Debtor had granted an interest in its inventory, the filed UCC-1 covered only inventory, and Debtor sold some inventory for cash, which it used to buy a piece of equipment. Under these circumstances, Creditor's automatic security interest in the equipment-proceeds would become unperfected on the 21st day after Debtor acquired the equipment unless Creditor filed a financing statement amendment as described above. If Debtor had traded the inventory *directly* for the equipment, section 9-315(d)(1) would provide perfection. A filed financing statement covered the original collateral (the inventory), and the proceeds are collateral in which a security interest can be perfected by filing in the same office (even though the original UCC-1 does not describe "equipment"). But since Debtor sold the inventory for cash and used the *cash proceeds* to purchase the equipment, § 9-315(d)(1) does not apply.

Another common situation in which § 9-315(d)(1) *does* apply is when a customer promises to pay for inventory later. Suppose Debtor from our example sold some inventory on credit to a customer who promised to pay for the inventory 30 days later (a common scenario among suppliers and distributors, for example). As discussed above, that promise to pay is an "account" (or an "instrument" if the customer signs a promissory note). Creditor has an automatically and continuously perfected security interest in that account as proceeds of the inventory. On the 21st day after Debtor sold the inventory, Creditor's interest would become unperfected were it not for § 9-315(d)(1) (as Creditor's UCC-1 does not describe "accounts"). But a filed financing statement covers the original inventory collateral, accounts are collateral in which a security interest can be perfected by filing in the same office, and the account was not acquired with cash proceeds. Thus, Creditor's security interest automatically attaches to and is perfected in the account (and when the customer pays on the account, Creditor will have an automatically and continuously perfected interest in the identifiable cash proceeds of the account). Once again, it does not matter under *this* test that the original UCC-1 does not mention "accounts."

Chains of proceeds for proceeds for proceeds like this can become quite confusing unless you focus on the link under analysis and how each of these four sets of conditions, including the three-part test of §9-315(d)(1), applies or does not apply. By the way, by definition, proceeds of collateral become "collateral" in their own right that can in turn produce proceeds, §9-102(a)(12)(A), although the point at which the "proceeds collateral" might become the "original collateral" mentioned in §9-315(d) is entirely unclear. Let us not further complicate an already complicated topic!

§6 Jurisdiction and Choice of Law (Conflicts) — Where to File

For property that does not move (e.g., land and buildings), choosing the state whose law governs secured transactions involving such property is simple and intuitive — the law of the state where the land is governs. For collateral that can and often does cross state lines, on the other hand, the choice of governing law is more complicated. As the introduction suggested, the rules in Article 9 are generally the same from state to state, although Louisiana in particular has adopted many non-uniform provisions. One rule that is different in *every* state, though, is the one indicating in which office one files a UCC-1 financing statement. As adopted by each state, §9-501 directs filers to the Secretary of State's office (or, in Louisiana, any parish clerk of court's office) in *that state*. But how does one choose which state's direction to follow, particularly if the collateral at issue is located in many different states?

The 2001 revision of Article 9 made resolution of this issue much clearer and easier. Under the new Article 9 as adopted in all states, the location of the *collateral* is in most cases irrelevant, as the law of the jurisdiction where the *debtor* is governs perfection, the effect of perfection, and the priority of a security interest in that debtor's collateral. §9-301(1). The rules establishing the *effect* of perfection and *priority* are quite uniform from state to state. Therefore, the central question for which this "choice of law" provision matters is where to file a financing statement. The general rule, then, is file in the state where the debtor is.

Two types of specific transactions are subject to different rules. First, for relatively rare "possessory" security interests (discussed above), in which perfection is accomplished by the creditor's holding possession of the collateral, the law of the state where the collateral is governs (in particular, the state law defining "possession"). §9-301(2). The same is true for security interests perfected by control, which are governed by the law of the state where, for example, the bank maintaining a deposit account or the broker maintaining a securities account is located. §§9-304, 9-305. The rules for what constitutes "possession" and "control," however, are not likely to vary significantly from state to state. Second, land-related interests, *see above* §3(d), are governed by the law of the state where the land is. Probably the most economically important of these transactions are ones involving pre-extraction interests in oil, gas, and other minerals ("as-extracted collateral"). Perfection of such interests is governed by the law of the state where the wellhead or minehead is. §9-301(4). Interests in standing timber subject to a recorded timber conveyance and in component parts of immovables are also governed by the law of the state where the land or other immovable is located. §9-301(3)(A)–(B).

Locating the debtor is sometimes more easily said than done. What about business debtors with several locations in several states—in which *one* governing state is such a debtor located? The revised Article 9 also answers this question. Individual debtors are located in the state of their "principal residence." §9-307(b)(1). This term is left undefined, although presumably most courts would adopt the "domicile" rules from tax or civil procedural law in cases where the debtor might arguably have no "principal" residence. Business debtors organized as "registered organizations," *see above* §3(a), are located in their state of registry. §9-307(e). For example, a Delaware corporation or LLC is located in Delaware, even if all of its offices, personnel, and assets are located in Louisiana. Finally, business associations that are not "registered organizations" are located in the state in which they conduct business (if only one) or, if they do business in more than one state, in the state where their "chief executive office" (however defined) is located. § 9-307(b)(2)–(3).

§ 7 Changes Affecting Perfection over Time

Another complicating factor in this area of the law (as opposed to mortgage law) is that Article 9 carefully regulates a number of potential changes that might occur with respect to the debtor and the collateral over time. Movement of debtors (and sometimes collateral) across state lines is a particularly troublesome change that affects, of course, only movable property. These changes affect the financing statement filed to perfect a security interest, either by rendering the information in the UCC-1 obsolete and/or misleading or by changing the governing law and making the office in which the UCC-1 was filed the wrong place for filing. This section brings together the four most common changes over time and the rules for how Article 9 reacts (or demands that the creditor react) to those changes.

(a) Change in Use of Collateral

First, the debtor might simply change the *use* of the collateral in a way that renders the description of the collateral in the financing statement inaccurate and misleading. For example, the debtor might take an item out of "inventory" and begin using it in its business, rendering it "equipment." *See above* § 1(b)(1)(C). Even if the UCC-1 only mentions "inventory," the security interest in the item of inventory now used as equipment will be unaffected in most cases. Changes in use of collateral have no effect on the effectiveness of a filed financing statement. § 9-507(b). But the financing statement must be filed in the proper place. One change of use that would pose a problem is if *car* inventory were put to use in a car dealer-debtor's business. Now, the problem is not only the description of collateral, but the wrong filing office (recall that security interests in cars in Louisiana must be perfected by filing with the office of motor vehicles, not in the UCC records, *see above* §4(a)). Such a change of use would require immediate action by the creditor to "re-perfect" the security interest by filing in a different office, and Article 9 offers no "grace period" for this problem.

(b) Debtor Name Changes (Including Post-Merger)

Second, recall that the most important piece of information on a financing statement is the debtor's name, as that information is used to index the security interest for later searchers. Under some circumstances, the debtor's name might change in a way that makes the financing statement "seriously misleading." For example, a woman might take on her new husband's last name, and a searcher looking for her new name in the UCC records might well not find a filing under her former name. The same could occur if a business officially changed its name on its organizational documents. This is a more serious problem, but it still has only a limited impact on the effectiveness of the now-misleading financing statement.

Changes in the debtor's name have no effect on the filing perfection of collateral acquired by the debtor before or within four months after the name change. §9-507(b)–(c)(1). So if Creditor has filed a financing statement to perfect an interest in Martha Jones's present and after-acquired equipment, Creditor's financing statement remains effective to perfect its interest in all of the equipment that Martha Jones owns on the day of her marriage (when she changes her name to Martha Stewart) and in any equipment Martha acquires during the next four months. Creditor's perfection will continue in this equipment indefinitely (at least until the UCC-1 expires, *see below* §7(d)). Note that this same rule applies to collateral that remains subject to a security interest following transfer to a third party under §9-315(a)(1). The new owner of the collateral is "the debtor" by definition, §9-102(a)(28)(A), and this "debtor's" name will likely be quite different from the original debtor's name. Nonetheless, the original UCC-1 filed in the previous debtor's name will remain effective against the collateral now owned by a "debtor" with a totally different name. It can be quite difficult for searchers to identify such security interests and locate the filings, but this is the compromise position that Article 9 establishes.

The other part of the compromise is that, unless the creditor amends the financing statement to reflect the debtor's new name, the now-misleading UCC-1 will be ineffective to perfect the creditor's security interest in any collateral acquired *after* this four-month grace period expires. §9-507(c)(2). So if Martha acquires an industrial stove for business purposes six months after her marriage and name change, Creditor's UCC-1 listing Martha's previous name will be ineffective to perfect Creditor's security interest in *this new* "equipment" (although, again, the interest in the older equipment remains perfected). The problem is most acute for inventory interests. Within a year or so after the debtor's name change, most or all of the inventory the debtor acquired before and shortly after the name change is likely to have been sold and replaced with new inventory. Unless the creditor amends the UCC-1 filed under the debtor's former name, this financing statement will be ineffective to perfect the creditor's interest in most or all of debtor's inventory (acquired after four months after the name change).

Debtors relatively rarely just change their names, but business debtors do merge with and into other companies, resulting in the debtor's property being owned by a different debtor with a new name. This is more substantial than simply transferring one item of collateral to a third party, who then becomes "the debtor" with respect to *that one* item of collateral (see above for discussion of this simple scenario). Section 9-508 deals with the broader scenario where another person and potentially *all* of their property becomes bound by the original security agreement. Such a person is called by the term of art "new debtor," designating two different types of persons. First, a "new debtor" is someone who becomes bound by the original debtor's security agreement, so a security interest arises in that person's property to the extent described in the security agreement. This might happen, for example, when a sole proprietor "incorporates" her business by transferring her business assets to a new shell corporation and having the corporation agree (by separate contract) to take on her business obligations, including loan and security agreements affecting business property. Second, a "new debtor" is someone who accedes generally to *all* of the original debtor's assets and obligations as a matter of contract or law (in a corporate merger or acquisition, for example). §§9-102(a)(56); 9-203(d).

When a "new debtor" becomes bound by the "original debtor's" security agreement, the financing statement naming the original debtor will likely become seriously misleading. The effect is exactly the same as if the original debtor had simply changed names. The old UCC-1 remains effective to perfect a security interest in all collateral acquired by the "new debtor" within four months after the name change, but it is ineffective to perfect interests in collateral acquired beyond this point (unless amended to name the "new debtor"). §9-508(b).

(c) Location of Debtor or Collateral Changes

Third, as discussed above, the law of the state where the debtor is determines in which office a financing statement must be filed to perfect a security interest. If the debtor moves across state lines (or if the collateral is transferred across state lines to a third party, who becomes "the debtor" with respect to that collateral), the financing statement filed in the first state's office will no longer fulfill the requirements of the new and now governing state's law. Article 9 requires the secured party to react to this change in much the same way as for debtor name changes, but the consequences of failing to react are much more severe.

If the original debtor moves to a different state, the creditor must refile a new financing statement in the new governing jurisdiction's filing office within four months of the move. If the creditor so refiles, perfection is continuous back to the date of the original filing in the old state. If the creditor fails to refile in the debtor's new state within four months, however, the original financing statement becomes ineffective to perfect the security interest in *any* of the debtor's property. Indeed, in most cases, the law will deem the financing statement *never* to have been filed at all. Against a "purchaser of the collateral for value" (including another secured creditor), the secured creditor loses perfection retroactively to the beginning of time (as if the interest had never been perfected). §9-316(a)(2), (b). In slight contrast, as against those who obtain rights in the collateral without giving value to the debtor, such as judicial lienholders or the debtor's bankruptcy trustee, the secured creditor loses perfection only from the expiration of the four-month period forward (prospectively). Of course, the creditor can refile a financing statement and re-perfect *after* the expiration of this four-month period, but in such a case the creditor's *priority* in the collateral ranks from the date of refiling, rather than from the date of the original filing (which is important for reasons discussed below in §8).

Similarly, recall that, when the debtor transfers the collateral to a third party, the security interest generally follows the collateral into the third party's hands, and the third party becomes "the debtor" *with respect to that collateral.* §9-315(a)(1). The perfection rules for the security interest in *that* collateral are determined by the current owner's ("debtor's") state's law. If the original debtor transfers collateral across state lines to a third party "debtor" in a different state, we have the same change in governing law problem. The rules for reacting to such a change are somewhat more lenient though. If the governing law changes as a result of collateral being transferred to a different "debtor" in a different state, the creditor has *one year* to discover this transfer and file *another* UCC-1 (in addition to the one still effective against the original debtor's other collateral) in the different debtor's state (in that new debtor's name, describing only the collateral transferred subject to the security interest). §9-316(a)(3). The consequences for failing to make this additional filing within the one-year period are the same as for the other "jurisdiction change" problem — the interest in the transferred collateral becomes unperfected altogether (retroactively or prospectively, depending upon the conflicting claimant).

In a particularly complex problem, this "collateral movement across state lines" issue might arise as a result of a merger or other business transformation, even if the collateral does not physically move! If a sole proprietor sells all of her business assets to a shell corporation organized under the laws of a different state, or if the debtor business entity merges into a different entity organized under the laws of a different state, the "new debtor" with respect to all of this collateral will now be located in a different state, even if the property remains in the same state. For example, to shield herself from potential liability, a sole proprietor operating solely in Louisiana might sell all of her business assets to a shell corporation organized under Delaware law. The sole proprietor might well continue to operate the business in Louisiana, but now "the debtor" is the corporation, which is located as a matter of law in its state of registry (Delaware). The governing law for perfecting an interest in these business assets is now Delaware law, so a secured creditor with an interest in this collateral must refile in Delaware to re-perfect its interest within one year of the asset sale to the corporation. The same would be true if a Louisiana corporation merged into a Delaware corporation. The "name change" rules discussed above with respect to such scenarios are thus subsumed by the "jurisdiction change" rule if the resulting entity is "located" in a different state, as perfection will be lost not only in property acquired after four months after the asset sale or merger, but as to *all* of the transferred collateral one year after the asset sale or merger.

One final note concerning collateral covered by a certificate of title (motor vehicles). Cars often cross state lines, as well, but the perfection rules for such collateral are different. As discussed above, security interests in cars are perfected in most states by notation of the security interest on the title certificate. If a car moves across state lines, trouble occurs for a perfected secured creditor only if another state motor vehicles office erroneously issues a new, "clean" certificate for the car, not indicating the secured creditor's interest. If this relatively rare problem occurs, the rule here is close to the rule for reacting to other jurisdictional changes. The secured creditor has four months to have its interest noted on the new "clean" certificate of title or it loses perfection as to purchasers of the car for value (but not at all as to conflicting claimants who have not given value, such as judicial lienholders or the bankruptcy trustee of the owner of the car). § 9-316(e); *see also* § 9-337. Note that this rule applies only to cars taken into states *other than* Louisiana. If the car is brought *into* this state, Louisiana law contains an inapplicable definition of "certificate of title" and an empty cross-reference due to the unique Louisiana perfection method for cars (*see above* § 4(a)), so the law does not affect cars brought into Louisiana. The former state's certificate of title law will continue to govern the interest in the car. § 9-303.

(d) Automatic Lapse of Filing Perfection, Continuation

Finally, a filed financing statement is effective on the UCC records for five years after filing. §515(a). Unless the financing statement is "continued," it lapses; that is, it expires and becomes ineffective. As against "purchasers of the collateral for value" (again, including other secured creditors), the law treats a lapsed statement as if it had *never* been filed. §9-515(c). Perfection lapses only *prospectively* against conflicting claimants who did not acquire rights in the collateral in exchange for value, such as judicial lienholders and the debtor's bankruptcy trustee.

To avoid this fate, the secured creditor must file a "continuation statement" (on a different simple form, also available from the Secretary of State's website), which continues the effectiveness of the original UCC-1 for another five years beyond the original lapse date. §9-515(e). *Note well:* This continuation filing must occur within a relatively narrow window. A continuation statement can be filed *only* within the six-month period preceding the five-year lapse point. §9-515(d). A continuation statement filed earlier than this is ineffective (apparently to discourage annual continuation filings by nervous creditors), as is a statement filed after lapse (because, after the lapse date, there is no longer any effective UCC-1 to continue). §9-510(c). In Louisiana, UCC-1 filings made with the office of motor vehicles to perfect interests in motor vehicles are perpetually effective. They need not be continued. §9-515(h).

§8 Priorities

As discussed in §3 above, more than one creditor or other claimant might obtain rights in the same item(s) of the debtor's collateral. The collateral might be so valuable that all claimants can be satisfied, but quite often, the claims exceed the value of the collateral. In such cases, the law must establish how to allocate the collateral's value (in whole or in part) among conflicting claims. In security device law generally, the approach is to arrange the claims in rank order of "priority." The claimant who has highest priority in each item of collateral gets paid up to the amount of its claim secured by that collateral, and only if higher ranking claims are paid in full do lower ranking claims take any value from the collateral. Security device law generally does not divide value "pro rata" or by any other "equalizing" scheme. Higher ranking ("senior") claims take all, leaving little or nothing for lower ranking ("junior" or "subordinate") claims.

Thus, the Article 9 scheme of arranging priorities among interests in movable collateral is of utmost importance to creditors and other claimants. It determines whether security devices in such collateral will ultimately achieve their goal and offer some reliable value to secured creditors. A number of different kinds of creditors and other claimants might have conflicting rights in the same collateral, and Article 9 prioritizes different claims differently. This section addresses each of the various claimants and their priority treatment under Article 9.

(a) Article 9 Secured Creditors v. Lien Creditors

Some claimants obtain rights in the collateral without the debtor's consent. The law directs that such rights arise, whether or not the debtor desires this result. Such creditors include judgment creditors enforcing judgments that the debtor has refused (or is unable) to pay, creditors conferring certain goods and services on the debtor for which the debtor has refused (or is unable) to pay, the Internal Revenue Service attempting to collect on the debtor's unpaid tax obligations, and the trustee in a bankruptcy case initiated by (or against) the debtor, who accedes as a matter of law to all of the debtor's property rights. This section discusses the general treatment and sometimes special rights of such "involuntary" claimants.

(1) Judicial "Lien Creditors"

As discussed in the introduction, creditors who have not contracted in advance for security devices are relegated to the ordinary judicial process to enforce their claims against the debtor's property. Such claimants can enforce money judgments (on any kind of obligation, conventional or delictual), for example, only through "writs" issued by the clerk of court and directing elements of the debtor's patrimony to be identified and turned over to the judgment creditor. In some cases, even before they obtain judgments, claimants with strong causes of action can "preserve" rights for later enforcement by obtaining a writ of "attachment" or "sequestration" pursuant to which the sheriff "reserves" identified property against which an eventual judgment can be enforced. More commonly, a creditor with a judgment in hand enforces it by obtaining a writ of "fieri facias," pursuant to which either the sheriff seizes property in the debtor's possession ("levy") or the judgment creditor directs third parties to turn over to the sheriff any property they are holding for the debtor ("garnishment"), such as the bank maintaining the debtor's deposit account. As soon as the sheriff seizes specific property belonging to the debtor, the judgment creditor now has rights in specific property and becomes a "lien creditor" with respect to that property. § 9-102(a)(52)(A). If the debtor declares (or is forced into) bankruptcy, the trustee in bankruptcy for that case is also technically a "lien creditor," § 9-102(a)(52)(C), but we will address the specific rights and powers of bankruptcy trustees below.

The relative priority of "lien creditors" and Article 9 secured creditors is thus measured as of the moment when the sheriff's seizure is complete. The rule in its simplest form is that, as of that moment, if the Article 9 security interest is perfected, it beats the later-in-time lien creditor's rights. If the security interest is not perfected, the lien creditor's rights are "first in time, first in right." § 9-317(a)(2)(A). This simple rule is subject to two exceptions.

First, recall that a security interest cannot be perfected until it has "attached." § 9-308(a). It might occur that the necessary step for perfection has been taken (e.g., filing), but one or more of the three requirements for attachment has not yet been met. For example, at the moment when the "lien creditor's" rights arise in collateral, the secured creditor might have filed a financing statement with respect to that collateral, but it might not yet have finally approved or disbursed the loan, or the security agreement might not yet have been authenticated, even though the parties had reached an agreement in principle. In such a case, if attachment had not occurred because the debtor had not yet authenticated a security agreement (or taken possession or control of the collateral), as required by § 9-203(b)(3), the lien creditor will win even if the security agreement ultimately does "attach." But if a security agreement had been authenticated, but attachment had not yet occurred because value had not yet been given, or the debtor did not at that point yet have rights in the collateral, the secured creditor will win if the value is ultimately given or the debtor obtains rights and the security interest attaches (and is simultaneously perfected pursuant to the already filed UCC-1) after the lien creditor's rights have arisen. §9-317(a)(2)(B).

Second, Article 9 generally gives preferential treatment to purchase-money security interests (PMSIs). The law encourages creditors to provide value (either credit sales or money loans) to debtors to acquire new property. As discussed above in §4(d), purchase-money security interests secure repayment of credits or loans that enable debtors to acquire the very collateral securing the purchase credit/loan. §9-103. As against a lien creditor, a purchase-money security interest perfected after the lien creditor's rights arise in the PMSI collateral will still beat the lien creditor if two conditions are met. The PMSI must have attached before the lien creditor's rights arose, and the PMSI must be perfected before or within 20 days after the debtor receives delivery of the PMSI collateral. §9-317(e). If a purchase-money lender decides to take a PMSI in the property purchased with its loan *after* a lien has arisen in that property, perfecting such an interest within 20 days of the debtor's receiving delivery will not elevate the PMSI above the lien creditor. The PMSI must be in place (attached) before the lien arises, in addition to being perfected within 20 days after the debtor takes delivery of the collateral.

(2) Statutory "Lienholders"—Privileged Creditors

Note that the definition of "lien creditor" in Article 9 describes only creditors whose "liens" arise as a result of the judicial process, such as the sheriff's seizure or a bankruptcy filing. It does *not* encompass creditors whose "liens" arise as a matter of law based on nonjudicial circumstances. Such creditors might be called "statutory" lien creditors, and in Louisiana, the proper term is "privileged" creditors. *See below* §15(a); §9-102(d)(9)–(10) (defining "lien" to mean "privilege," and thus "lienholder" to mean a creditor with a privilege).

Chapter 3 of this book deals in great detail with the variety of statutory and codal "privileges" that Louisiana law confers on various creditors. Article 9 generally has little to say about conflicts between such privileged creditors and Article 9 secured creditors. *See below* §20. Nonetheless, a brief mention of privileged creditors is in order here.

Article 9 does specifically address the priority of one kind of privilege— "possessory liens." If a privilege in movable property secures repayment of an obligation for services or materials furnished with respect to that property, and the privilege depends on the claimant's possession of the property, then such a "possessory lien" has priority even over a prior perfected Article 9 security interest unless the privilege statute provides otherwise. §9-333. Perhaps the most common example of such a "possessory lien" is the privilege granted by law to automobile mechanics in the cars they repair to secure payment of their fees and expenses for parts and labor (the privilege exists only so long as the mechanic retains possession of the car, or for a short time after possession is released). The statute providing for such liens specifically provides that a prior perfected security interest beats the lien. La. Rev. Stat. 9:4501(B). The Civil Code article providing a similar but slightly narrower privilege, however, does not "provide otherwise," so the mechanic's "artisan's privilege" trumps even a prior perfected Article 9 security interest. Civ. C. art. 3217(2).

This and other possessory privileges (as well as non-possessory privileges) are discussed below in Chapter 3, but bear in mind for now that Article 9 security interests will generally enjoy higher priority than such liens. Louisiana law generally places Article 9 at the top of the security device ladder. More often than not, a properly perfected Article 9 security interest will beat *any* conflicting privilege, and even an *unperfected* Article 9 security interest will beat most privileges. §9-322(h); La. Rev. Stat. 9:4770. Some statutes specifically elevate certain privileges over a prior perfected security interest (*see, e.g.,* La. Rev. Stat. 9:5001, concerning attorneys' charging liens on recovered property), but these are quite rare.

(3) The Special Case of the IRS and Federal Tax Liens

One type of "statutory lien" deserves special mention, as it arises under *federal* statutory law, which trumps any inconsistent state law. The rules regulating the interplay between Article 9 security interests and federal tax liens are exceedingly complex. This book will address only the basics. Creditors and their lawyers are well advised to consult a tax specialist if tax liens are a major source of concern.

Federal tax law identifies the point in time at which the IRS tax lien "arises in" (attaches to) *all* of the debtor's property. This point is of relatively little significance to secured creditors, however, as federal law makes the IRS's lien effective against third-party creditors only after a notice of the tax lien has been filed in the proper office. For movable property, such notices are generally filed in the UCC records, just like financing statements.

In most cases, the priority rules are quite simple. The IRS tax lien loses (is subordinate to) a security interest perfected before the filing of the tax lien notice, and it beats (is senior to) any security interest perfected after the notice of tax lien has been filed. This simple rule is subject to two important exceptions.

First, with respect to *after-acquired* collateral, the IRS tax lien receives special treatment through a doctrine known as "choateness" (pronounced "KOE-ate-ness"). Recall that a security interest can attach and be perfected in property only after the debtor has present rights in the property; that is, the debtor's rights in specific collateral must be "choate" before the creditor's interest can attach and be perfected in that collateral. §9-203(b)(2). The IRS tax lien is not subject to this limitation. As soon as its notice of tax lien is filed, the IRS's lien is deemed effective even against the debtor's *inchoate* future rights in property acquired after the filing. Therefore, the IRS's lien will generally beat a perfected security interest in any property the debtor acquires *after* the filing of the notice of tax lien. The tax lien statute contains exceptions to this rule for perfected security interests in certain collateral ("commercial financing security," including inventory) acquired within 45 days after notice of the tax lien was filed, but the labyrinthine statute providing for this exception is far too complex to be analyzed in detail here. *See* 26 U.S.C. §6323(c). Bear in mind simply that an IRS tax lien will prevail with respect to almost all after-acquired collateral.

Second, if the secured creditor advances value to the debtor (expecting that an already perfected security interest will secure this "future" value, §9-204(c)) after notice of the tax lien has been filed, the IRS might prevail over the security interest to the extent that it secures this later value. If the secured creditor extends this later value *knowing* that the tax lien notice has been filed, its claim to security for *that value* will lose to the IRS's lien. Even if the secured creditor is unaware of the tax lien notice filing, however, security interests securing value advanced after 45 days after filing of the tax lien notice are subordinated to the IRS's lien in any event. 26 U.S.C. §6323(d).

To illustrate both of these rules, suppose that Creditor has a perfected security interest in Debtor's "present and after-acquired" equipment, securing "any and all indebtedness owing from Debtor to Creditor, arising from any source whatsoever and arising at any time in the past, present, or future." On day X, Creditor has advanced $10,000 of value to Debtor, and Debtor owns $9,000 of equipment. Suppose further that, on day X+100, the IRS files a notice of tax lien against Debtor for $3,000 in unpaid back taxes. On day X+120, Debtor acquires $3,000 more equipment, and on day X+150, Creditor advances an additional $2,000 to Debtor. Creditor believes that its now $12,000 claim against Debtor will be secured by the now $12,000 in old and new equipment pursuant to the original security agreement. Creditor correctly understands the effect of its security agreement against Debtor, but *some of* its rights will be subordinated to the IRS tax lien in Debtor's equipment for two reasons. First, with respect to the $3,000 of equipment acquired after the IRS tax lien notice had been filed, the "choateness" doctrine ensures that the IRS lien will be superior to Creditor's prior perfected security interest. The IRS's lien is deemed to have been effective against the new $3,000 of equipment from the moment when its notice was filed (on day X+100), while Creditor's security interest is deemed to have been effective only from the moment when Debtor actually acquired the equipment (20 days later, on day X+120). The IRS's lien is thus first in time, first in right, and its claim takes the entire $3000 value of the new collateral. In addition, even if Debtor had acquired the entire

$12,000 of equipment before day X+100, because Creditor made the future advance beyond 45 days after the tax lien notice had been filed, its interest securing the $2,000 future loan would be subordinated to the IRS's lien in any event. Creditor would have the priority interest securing its original $10,000 loan, but the IRS's $3,000 lien would displace Creditor's security interest securing the $2,000 future loan. If the IRS's claim could be paid off, Creditor's remaining claim would stand in third priority, but the collateral here is sufficient only to cover the IRS's claim.

(4) Special Rules for Future Advances

With respect to *future* advances of value by secured creditors, "lien creditors" can prevail over prior perfected security interests in much the same way as the IRS's tax lien prevails over future advances, as described immediately above. Generally, a prior perfected security interest will beat a "lien creditor's" interest in collateral regardless of when the secured value was advanced or when the debtor acquired the collateral. But a lien creditor whose rights arise in collateral after a secured creditor has properly perfected a competing interest in that collateral will prevail over the secured creditor's claim under a very narrow set of circumstances. A lien creditor's claim is superior to a competing security interest to the extent that the security interest secures value advanced *both* after 45 days after the lien arose in the collateral at issue *and* with actual knowledge of the existence of the lien (unless the creditor made the loan pursuant to an earlier *binding commitment* to make the loan). §9-323(b).

To illustrate, suppose that Creditor has a perfected security interest in Debtor's "present and after-acquired" equipment, securing "any and all indebtedness owing from Debtor to Creditor, arising from any source whatsoever and arising at any time in the past, present, or future." On day X, Creditor has advanced $9,000 of value to Debtor, and Debtor owns $10,000 of equipment. Suppose further that, on day X+100, Lien Creditor sends the sheriff to seize ("levy on") a $1,000 piece of equipment belonging to Debtor. On day X+150, Debtor requests a $1,000 loan from Creditor. Debtor explains that this $1000 loan will bring Creditor's total claim to $10,000, which would be totally secured by Debtor's $10,000 in equipment. Debtor further explains that the purpose of the advance is, at least in part, to use friendly Creditor's superior rights to protect the extra $1,000 in equipment from hostile Lien Creditor's efforts to enforce its lien in that equipment. If Creditor makes the loan, its security interest will be subordinated to Lien Creditor's rights (and Debtor's scam will be foiled). This is the very specific scenario that the law apparently seeks to avoid. Creditor will have made a secured advance *both* beyond 45 days after the lien had arisen in the collateral *and* with knowledge of the lien's existence. Note that, unlike with respect to the IRS's lien, if *either* of these factors is not met, the secured creditor's claim remains superior to the lien creditor's, even with respect to the future loan.

(5) The Trustee in Bankruptcy

One of the most important reasons—if not *the* most important reason—why most creditors take security interests is to avoid or minimize the potential negative effects of their debtors' bankruptcy. Having a reserved interest in identified property powerfully enhances secured creditors' rights in bankruptcy and elevates them far above the rights of unsecured creditors. Bankruptcy recoveries for secured creditors are often quite handsome, while the recoveries of their unsecured counterparts are meager in most cases. The trustee in bankruptcy ("TIB") appointed to oversee the debtor's property (or in some cases, the "debtor in possession" managing its own property) represents these unsecured creditors. Therefore, one of the TIB's primary occupations is to do everything possible to destroy the special rights of secured creditors and bring their collateral into the estate to increase the distribution to unsecured creditors (and, consequently, to increase the TIB's commission). Federal bankruptcy law gives the TIB two primary tools to destroy security interests. These tools bring value into the estate from other sources, as well, but the discussion below will be limited to their application against secured creditors.

(A) Strong-Arm

The TIB is also technically a "lien creditor," §9-102(a)(52)(C), so the first tool derives from the simple test for ranking all "lien creditors" against secured creditors. As of the moment of the bankruptcy filing, if the Article 9 security interest is perfected, it beats the later-in-time TIB's rights and survives. If the security interest is not perfected, the TIB's rights are "first in time, first in right." §9-317(a)(2)(A). As a result, the TIB can exercise its superior rights in the collateral for the benefit of the unsecured creditors. 11 U.S.C. §544(a)(1). In effect, the TIB can all but destroy the security interest, rendering the secured creditor effectively unsecured.

(B) Preferences

Even if a security interest is perfected on "bankruptcy day," the TIB might still be able to destroy it on the basis that it represents an unfair "preference" for the secured creditor made during the sensitive period shortly before the debtor's bankruptcy filing. The topic of preferences in bankruptcy is highly technical and quite complicated, but with respect to security interests, only a few points need to be examined.

First, the TIB must establish that the debtor's granting of the security interest constituted a "preferential transfer." The debtor's granting a security interest always represents "a transfer of an interest of the debtor in property to or for the benefit of a creditor," 11 U.S.C. §547(b)(1), and having a security interest virtually always allows the creditor to receive more than the creditor would receive in a liquidation without the security interest, 11 U.S.C. §547(b)(5), so any security interest might constitute a *preferential* transfer if meets three additional requirements. The transfer must have occurred (1) "on account of an antecedent debt," (2) while the debtor was insolvent, and (3) within 90 days of the debtor's bankruptcy filing (or one year, if the creditor is an "insider," which is relatively seldom the case). 11 U.S.C. §547(b)(2)–(4). The debtor is presumed to have been insolvent during the 90 days preceding its bankruptcy filing, 11 U.S.C. §547(f), and this presumption is quite difficult to rebut, so the second and third tests largely overlap. And a transfer is "on account of an antecedent debt" simply if the debt arose before the transfer occurred. Thus, these final three tests all turn on the *timing* of the transfer of the security interest.

For security interests, the timing of attachment and especially perfection establish the timing of the "transfer" (and thus whether or not the "preferential transfer" test is met). As a matter of law, the transfer of a security interest is deemed to have occurred when it was perfected, unless it was perfected within 30 days after attachment, in which case the transfer is deemed to have occurred at attachment. 11 U.S.C. § 547(e)(2) (note that, before October 2005, this "grace period" was only 10 days). Note that this "grace period" extends *beyond* the day of the bankruptcy filing. Creditors are specifically allowed to perfect their security interests even *after* the bankruptcy filing if they are trying to take advantage of this 30-day perfection period. 11 U.S.C. § 362(b)(3).

Thus, if the last of the three requirements for attachment occurred on day X, but the security interest was not perfected (e.g., by filing) until day X+31, the transfer will be deemed to have occurred on day X+31. As a result, the transfer is more likely to fall within the 90-day pre-bankruptcy preference period, and the debt (probably arising on day X) will certainly predate the transfer (on day X+31). On the other hand, if the security interest was perfected on day X+21, the transfer will be deemed to have occurred "retroactively" on day X, at attachment, which may fall beyond 90 days before the bankruptcy filing, and the transfer on day X might well have been contemporaneous with (not antecedent to) the debt (probably also arising on day X). If the security interest was granted to secure pre-existing indebtedness, the "transfer" will always be "on account of an antecedent debt," but perfection within 30 days of attachment might still place the transfer outside the critical 90-day pre-bankruptcy period.

Even if the security interest meets these criteria, the law excepts some preferential transfers from attack by the TIB. Recall that timely perfected purchase-money security interests (PMSIs) generally receive favorable treatment (*see above* §§ 4(d), 8(a)(1)). This is true also in bankruptcy. All PMSIs perfected within 30 days of the debtor's receiving delivery of the collateral are immune from later attack by the TIB. 11 U.S.C. § 547(c)(3) (note that the perfection period here was increased from 20 days as of October 17, 2005). Note that, although *any* security interest perfected within 30 days of *attachment* might escape being categorized as a preferential transfer altogether, the PMSI-exception period is measured from the debtor's *receipt of the collateral*, which might occur well after attachment of the security interest. Recall that PMSIs in consumer goods are automatically perfected, so any PMSI in a consumer good should escape later "preference" attack by the consumer-debtor's TIB.

(b) Article 9 Secured Creditors v. Buyers/Lessees of Collateral

Recall from §5 that security interests generally follow collateral into the hands of third parties to whom the debtor has transferred the collateral. §9-315(a)(1). Of course, the secured creditor can essentially waive this benefit by authorizing the transfer *free and clear* of the security interest, but sometimes the security interest is cut off (and the third party recipient "wins" with respect to the creditor) even without the creditor's consent. This section discusses the three most common such situations.

(1) Unperfected Security Interests (and Future Advances)

A consistent theme in security device law generally holds that "secret liens" are not enforceable against third parties. Article 9 carries forward that theme by subordinating unperfected security interests to conflicting third party's rights in the same collateral. *See, e.g.,* §8(a)(1), (a)(5)(A). This rule applies to most buyers and lessees of collateral, as well. If a security interest is not perfected when a buyer or lessee has *both* given value for *and* taken delivery of the collateral *without knowledge of the security interest,* the buyer or lessee takes the collateral free of the security interest. §9-317(b)–(c). This is a consistent rule embodying a simple principle: perfect your security interest, or lose its advantages against uninformed third parties who perfect their rights.

Even a perfected security interests might be subordinated to the rights of buyers and lessees to the extent that the security interest secures value given after the sale or lease. The rule here is virtually identical to the rule with respect to the IRS's tax lien and future advances. *See above* §8(a)(3). If the secured creditor advances value to the debtor *either* with knowledge that the sale/lease to the third party has occurred *or* after 45 days after the sale/lease becomes enforceable by the third party, the security interest securing *that advance* (but not the perfected security interest securing *prior* advances) is subordinate to the rights of the buyer/lessee. §9-323(d)–(g). Here again, this rule only applies to *discretionary* future advances; it does not apply to loans made pursuant to an earlier *binding commitment* to make future loans.

(2) Buyers In Ordinary Course of Business

Certain buyers of collateral receive a blanket exception to the rule that security interests follow collateral after disposition. To facilitate modern retailing operations, the law automatically removes even perfected security interests from collateral sold in the ordinary course of the debtor's business. §9-320(a).

Only "buyers in ordinary course of business" benefit from this special rule. To fall within this defined term, the buyer and the transaction must meet three requirements. §1-201(9) [§1-201(b)(9) in the soon-to-be-revised version of Article 1]. First, the buyer must purchase the collateral in good faith without knowledge that the purchase violates some other person's rights in the collateral. This vaguely requires that the buyer be acting honestly and not with an intention to harm the secured creditor. §1-201(19) [§1-201(b)(20) in revised Article 1]. The buyer can know that the collateral is subject to the security interest, but the buyer must not know that the sale *violates* the secured creditor's rights in the collateral. Note that the sale might well indeed *not* violate the secured creditor's rights (unless the security agreement prohibits sales without the creditor's permission), but few third parties would have any reason to know about any violation in any event. Second, the consideration for the sale must be something other than total or partial satisfaction of a pre-existing money debt owed by the debtor-seller to the buyer. The buyer has to give new value in the form of present payment or a promise of future payment. Third and finally, the debtor-seller must be "in the business of selling goods of that kind," and the sale to the buyer must comport with ordinary business practices in the industry, or at least with the debtor-seller's ordinary business practices. In other words, the collateral must be "inventory" in the debtor-seller's hands; sales of the debtor's "equipment" are excluded. Also excluded are "fire sales," bulk sales, "going-out-of-business sales," and other sales that differ from the debtor-seller's ordinary sales practices.

Even a "buyer in ordinary course of business" will not take free of a perfected security interest unless three other requirements are met. First, the debtor-seller must not be a person engaged in farming operations. The federal Food Security Act sets up a very similar regime for buyers of farmers' inventory in 7 U.S.C. §1631, so §9-320(a) is pre-empted by this federal rule. Second, the inventory must not be in the creditor's possession. §9-320(e). If the creditor has set up a "field warehouse" or is otherwise in actual or constructive possession of the collateral, buyers in ordinary course of business cannot take free of possessory security interests.

Finally, the security interest must have been "created by the buyers' seller." That is, buyers in ordinary course of business do *not* take free of security interests that were created by their seller's *predecessor(s)* and that followed the collateral into the seller's hands. For example, suppose Previous Owner granted a security interest in his car to Bank, and Bank properly perfected that interest. Suppose further that Previous Owner later sold the car to Used Car Dealer, but he did not pay off the secured car loan with the sale proceeds. The car in Used Car Dealer's hands remains subject to Bank's security interest (which was "created" — that is, granted — by Previous Owner). §9-315(a)(1). If Buyer purchases the car from Used Car Dealer, Buyer cannot benefit from §9-320(a) and avoid Bank's security interest, even though he is a "buyer in ordinary course of business." The security interest at issue was "created" by Previous Owner, not by "Buyer's seller," Used Car Dealer. Therefore, §9-320(a) does not apply, and Buyer would own the car still subject to Bank's security interest.

(3) The "Garage-Sale" Exception

To protect consumers who buy used goods from other consumers, the law provides one more narrow exception to the rule that security interests follow collateral after sale. Recall that purchase-money security interests in consumer goods (other than motor vehicles) are automatically perfected. §9-309(1). If the consumer-debtor then resells the used collateral to another consumer (in a "garage sale" or similar informal transaction), the buyer has very little opportunity to discover that she is buying goods subject to a perfected security interest. Of course, the buyer could simply ask the seller, but consumer buyers are unlikely to perceive the *possibility* of a security interest following goods into their hands.

Article 9 strikes a compromise in such situations. Because consumers buying goods from other consumers are not "buyers in ordinary course of business," security interests perfected *by filing* follow consumer-goods collateral into the hands of such "garage sale" buyers. §9-320(b)(4). But consumer buyers take free of security interests in consumer goods not perfected by filing before the consumer-to-consumer sale. So long as the seller bought or used the goods primarily for personal, family, or household use, and the buyer intends to use the goods for similar purposes, the buyer takes free of security interests not perfected by filing as soon as the buyer gives value for the goods. §9-320(b)(2)–(3). This rule does not apply to "possessory" security interests, §9-320(e), but creditors seldom remain in possession of consumer-goods collateral.

(c) Priority Among Article 9 Secured Creditors

The rules for resolving conflicts among Article 9 secured creditors are fairly predictable, simple, and straightforward. Real complications arise only with respect to purchase-money security interests in inventory (and its proceeds), and even then, the "exceptional" rules are relatively simple.

(1) General Rules

Following a clear trend already established, unperfected security interests lose to perfected security interests. §9-322(a)(2). If both secured creditors have failed to properly perfect their interests, the first security interest to have attached to the collateral wins. §9-322(a)(3). Such situations would presumably be quite rare, however, as the first creditor to realize that its interest is not properly perfected might still be able to rush to the courthouse and perfect its interest by filing (and thus beat its still unperfected rival). As between two properly perfected security interests, the first in time to have either filed a financing statement covering the collateral or perfected an interest in the collateral wins. Note that the rule focuses on *whichever* action—filing or perfection—occurred first, and recall that one cannot perfect a security interest before it has attached, but one can "pre-file" with the debtor's authorization to preserve priority for later.

For example, suppose Bank One and Debtor begin negotiations for a secured loan on day X. On that day, Debtor authorizes Bank One to file a financing statement against Debtor's "inventory, equipment, and accounts," and Bank does so. Bank has no security interest to perfect; it is simply reserving its priority if it eventually makes a secured loan to Debtor. Negotiations drag on, so Debtor secretly approaches Bank Two with a similar request for a secured loan. Bank Two immediately agrees to make the loan, secured by Debtor's inventory. On day X+30, Debtor authenticates a promissory note and security agreement granting Bank Two a security interest in its inventory, and Bank Two advances a $25,000 loan to Debtor and files a financing statement against Debtor's "inventory." Three weeks later, on day X+51, Bank One and Debtor finally reach agreement. Bank One searches the UCC-1 filings and finds Bank Two's filing, but it goes forward with the deal nonetheless. Debtor authenticates a promissory note and security agreement granting Bank One a security interest in its inventory, and Bank Two advances a $25,000 loan to Debtor. If Debtor defaults on both loans, and its inventory is only worth $25,000 (note that, despite what its UCC-1 suggests, Bank One has no security interest in Debtor's equipment and accounts, as only the security agreement can create rights), Bank One has priority. Even though Bank Two's security interest attached and was perfected before Bank One even had a security interest, Bank One *filed* before Bank Two *perfected*. Therefore, even though Bank One went forward despite Bank Two's already perfected interest, Bank One has priority. First to file *or* perfect first wins, *whichever* is first.

(2) Exceptions for Alternative Perfection Methods

Under certain circumstances, the "first-in-time" rule is suspended, and a security interest perfected *later* can beat a *prior* perfected security interest. The first set of exceptions applies to security interests perfected other than by filing a financing statement (e.g., by possession or control). First, security interests in "instruments" perfected by possession beat all other interests not perfected by possession as long as the "purchaser" (including a secured creditor) gives value and perfects by taking possession in good faith without notice that the "purchase" (i.e., the secured loan) violates the rights of an earlier-perfected secured party. §9-330(d) (*see also* §9-330(a)–(c) with respect to chattel paper). Second, a security interest perfected by control will beat all other interests not perfected by control. §§9-327(1) (deposit accounts); 9-328(1) (investment property); 9-329(1) (letter-of-credit rights); 9-329.1(2) (life insurance policies). Two control-perfected security interests generally rank according to the first in time to obtain control. §§9-327(2); 9-328(2); 9-329(2); 9-329.1(3). However, the security interest of the bank, securities intermediary (broker-dealer), or insurance company with control over collateral maintained by such entities take priority over other control-perfected security interests. §§9-327(3)–(4) (deposit accounts, but not if the competing creditor established control by becoming the bank's customer with respect to the account), 9-328(3); 9-329.1(1).

(3) PMSI Exceptions

The second set of exceptions to the "first-in-time" rule applies to purchase-money security interests. Following another clearly established trend, the law favors creditors who give value to debtors and take and timely perfect purchase-money security interests (PMSIs) in the collateral acquired with their secured credit. Generally, PMSIs perfected within 20 days after the debtor receives possession of the collateral beat all other security interests in that collateral and in its proceeds (perhaps subject to the rights of those with "control" over deposit accounts, §9-327). §9-324(a). Note that this exception is broader than the PMSI exception with respect to lien creditors, which applies only if the PMSI attached before the lien creditor's rights arose in the collateral. *See above* §8(a)(1). Here, a PMSI perfected within 20 days of delivery of the collateral to the debtor beats *any* other security interest, even one that attached before the PMSI did. In the rare case in which more than one creditor has a PMSI in the same collateral, a credit seller's PMSI beats a purchase-money lender's PMSI (and in other cases, first to file or perfect wins). §9-324(g).

If the collateral is inventory, and if a conflicting security interest in that inventory is perfected by filing before the PMSI is perfected, §9-324(c), two more requirements must be fulfilled for the PMSI to enjoy super-priority over the prior-perfected security interest. First, the PMSI has to be perfected before the debtor-buyer receives possession of the inventory collateral. §9-324(b)(1). The 20-day grace period is eliminated. Second, also before the debtor takes delivery of the collateral, the conflicting non-PMSI creditor must receive "authenticated notification" (generally a signed letter, but perhaps an email, etc.) from the PMSI creditor describing the debtor's inventory and stating that the PMSI creditor "has or expects to acquire" a PMSI in that inventory. §9-324(b)(2)–(4). This one notification can satisfy the notice requirement as against the competing non-PMSI creditor for PMSIs granted to the PMSI creditor over the next five years. §9-324(b)(3). A similar set of rules applies to PMSIs in livestock. §9-324(d)–(e).

In addition, with respect to PMSI super-priority in the *proceeds* of *inventory* collateral, there is an exception to the exception to the exception. Generally, PMSI priority in collateral extends to the identifiable proceeds of that collateral, too. §9-324(a). For the proceeds of *inventory*, however, PMSI super-priority flows only into proceeds that are "chattel paper or an instrument" or "cash proceeds ... to the extent ... received on or before the delivery of the inventory to a buyer." §9-324(b). Intentionally excluded here are "accounts" that are the proceeds of inventory. If inventory is sold on credit (and no promissory note is executed), the rules for priority in those accounts are the basic first-to-file-or-perfect rules for all security interests. A competing non-PMSI creditor will likely have filed or perfected first and will thus have priority over the purchase-money creditor in the *proceeds* of inventory, unless the proceeds are either cash or a check received immediately upon sale, or the buyer signs a promissory note. § 9-322(b)(1).

(d) Article 9 Interests in Component Parts ("Fixtures") v. Mortgagees

Because of the very nature of the property involved, security interests in movables seldom come into conflict with mortgages and other interests in immovables. But as discussed above in § 3(d), some movables become attached (affixed) to, and thus become part of, immovable property, giving rise to a potential conflict between those with security rights in the movable (component part or "fixture") and those with mortgage and other rights in the immovable. Article 9 generally resolves such conflicts in favor of the immovable rights holder (either the mortgagee or the subsequent owner of the immovable). § 9-334(c). Under a few circumstances, though, an Article 9 security interest in a fixture can prevail. This section describes those circumstances.

With respect to one particularly important "land-related" interest, Article 9 always trumps mortgage interests: unharvested crops. Because crops in which a security interest has been granted are "movable by anticipation," it may be that the mortgagee of the farmland has no interest in the crops (at least as a matter of mortgage law). But to eliminate any doubt, Article 9 confirms that a perfected security interest in crops beats any conflicting interest of a mortgagee or later owner of the farmland (so long as the debtor-farmer has an interest of record in the land). § 9-334(i).

With respect to movables that become attached to immovable property, a mortgage or other interest in an immovable generally extends to its component parts. Civ. C. art. 469. If a movable good to which an Article 9 security interest has attached is later affixed to an immovable, the mortgagee or subsequent owner of the immovable will have priority over the Article 9 secured creditor in the "component part" unless one of three conditions is met.

First, consistent with basic "first to file" principles, if the Article 9 fixture interest is properly perfected by fixture filing before the immovable property interest is recorded, the fixture interest will have priority. §9-334(e)(1). Note that, if any immovable interest holder establishes priority over the fixture interest holder, it can pass on its priority under the "shelter principle," and the fixture interest will remain subordinate to the transferee's rights, even if recorded later. §9-334(e)(1)(B).

Second, a fixture interest can obtain priority even over a prior-recorded immovable interest holder if the security interest is a PMSI and is perfected by fixture filing before the fixture is affixed. §9-334(d). If the competing immovable rights holder has a prior-recorded *construction* mortgage (in a sense, the equivalent of a purchase-money interest to finance improvement or construction of an immovable), the construction mortgagee will beat even a PMSI as to fixtures affixed during the construction. §9-334(h). Outside Louisiana, this "PMSI exception" operates much like the exception with respect to lien creditors and secured creditors, in that the PMSI creditor has 20 days after the fixture becomes part of the immovable to perfect. Louisiana's rule is non-uniform here. After a movable good becomes affixed to an immovable, no unperfected Article 9 security interest can be perfected *or even maintained* in the now-component part. A fixture interest, including a PMSI, *must* be perfected by fixture filing *before* the good is affixed to the immovable.

Finally, a fixture interest can prevail over conflicting rights in the immovable if the immovable rights holder in an authenticated record consents to the security interest or disclaims any interest in the fixture. §9-334(f)(1). Of course, if the debtor can legally remove the fixture without the consent of the conflicting immovable rights holder, the fixture security interest holder can exercise this right, as well. §9-334(f)(2).

One final point about Louisiana's non-uniform law. Outside Louisiana, a security interest in a fixture perfected by a method other than a "fixture filing" beats a subsequent interest acquired by judicial proceedings (including the trustee in bankruptcy's rights). §9-334(e)(3). Although this section is not "[reserved]" in the Louisiana law, it has no application here, as security interests in fixtures can be perfected *only* by fixture filing. Any other method of perfection (such as a non-fixture filing) is wholly ineffective. §9-334(a) and official comments.

§9 Enforcement Remedies

In most cases, security devices simply act as a sort of insurance for the creditor, and no "claim" on that insurance is ever made. The great majority of secured obligations are fulfilled, either according to the original contract, or pursuant to a restructured settlement agreement (in which case the security device will have provided leverage to enhance the creditor's bargaining position in reaching a satisfactory settlement). In some cases, though, the debtor is in no position to perform (or adamantly refuses to perform), and the creditor seeks to enforce the security device to fulfill the obligation with the value of the collateral. The enforcement process comprises at least three stages: (1) the debtor's default, (2) repossession of the collateral from the debtor or a third party, and (3) either the debtor's full payment and "redemption" of the collateral or foreclosure of the debtor's redemption right through disposition of the collateral, followed by distribution of the proceeds to the creditor to cover the unpaid obligation. Both Part 6 of Article 9 (the sections numbered 9-6XX) and the Code of Civil Procedure impose a myriad of detailed requirements and restrictions on the enforcement process. This section describes only the highlights and the general contours of the process as regulated by Article 9, particularly the significantly non-uniform Louisiana law governing repossession.

(a) Default

A security device may be enforced only after the debtor defaults on the principal obligation. Most generally, "default" simply signifies failure of the debtor to perform the obligation as agreed. Missing one or more payments when payment becomes due is clearly a default (at least as to the obligation to make those installment payments). Default can and often does encompass much more than this, however.

Indeed, something a third party does, or a general downturn in the economy, might signal a default. The law has very little to say about what can or does constitute "default." Instead, the nature and scope of this central concept is left to the parties to define as a matter of contract. Most sophisticated commercial security agreements and loan agreements include a long list of "events of default," often including such things as failure to maintain a certain level of general profitability, failure to provide periodic reports of economic performance, or even having a third-party tenant who defaults on its obligation. The law generally takes a rather "laissez-faire" approach to the parties' defining "default" for their transaction (although see the discussion in the immediately following section regarding Louisiana's unique motor vehicle repossession law and its definition of default).

(b) Repossession

If the creditor chooses to enforce its security interest in the debtor's collateral, it must gain dominion over that collateral, usually in preparation for a sale or other disposition. Sometimes the creditor can obtain the necessary control over collateral without involving the debtor at all. A creditor with a "possessory" security interest, for example, *see above* § 2(c)(1), will already be in possession of the collateral, although such cases are the rare exception. In a more common situation, if the collateral is an account, deposit account, or other third-party obligation, no confrontation with the debtor is required to collect the value of such collateral (although summary process might be necessary to take possession of "instruments" or other documentation of such an obligation, § 9-607(f)). The creditor can simply notify the third-party obligor ("account debtor"), such as the bank or a customer who owes money to the debtor, to direct payment or other performance to the creditor rather than to the debtor. § 9-607. The only requirement of this simple process is that the creditor act in a "commercially reasonable" manner in collecting from account debtors. Of course, the creditor can collect and keep only so much of the third-party obligation as will cover the secured obligation and any collection expenses. The debtor is entitled to any "surplus." § 9-608(a).

In many cases, though, the debtor will be in possession of tangible collateral, and the creditor must physically divest the debtor of possession. In other words, the creditor must "repossess" the collateral from the debtor. This process can and often does evoke significant antagonism on the part of the debtor, sometimes leading to angry or even violent confrontations. Louisiana law seeks to defuse such potentially explosive situations by placing public authorities in almost exclusive control of the process of repossession. This differs substantially from the creditor-directed approach of Article 9 as adopted by most other states.

In most places outside Louisiana, § 9-609(a) allows the secured creditor to repossess the collateral (or render it immobile or unusable), either personally or through a repossession agent, by any means, so long as the private repossession proceeds "without breach of the peace." In these states, Article 9 eliminates conversion and theft liability for self-help repossession of the collateral. Theoretically, the ability to move quickly and decisively with respect to the collateral, without inefficient and expensive intervention by public authorities, is a major advantage of being a secured creditor. Practically, though, self-help repossession is a mine field for creditors and their agents confronted with all manner of opposition from debtors. Each state has a line of jurisprudence exploring what does and does not constitute a "breach of the peace," and the answers often differ substantially from place to place. Debtors have won large verdicts against creditors found to have breached the peace, and the simple fact of having to defend countless lawsuits charging a breach makes self-help repossession a mixed blessing. Creditors outside Louisiana engage in self-help repossession at their own risk.

For collateral located in Louisiana, in contrast, most creditors are strictly prohibited from engaging in self-help repossession (even out-of-state creditors enforcing security interests in collateral located here). Under Louisiana's version of § 9-609(a), creditors can take possession of the collateral from the debtor in only three ways: First, the debtor can abandon or surrender the collateral to the creditor voluntarily. Second, the debtor can consent to the creditor's private repossession, but only "after or in contemplation of default." § 9-609(a)(2). Finally, if the debtor refuses to cooperate, the creditor must use judicial process to have the sheriff seize the collateral. This does not mean the creditor must proceed through the long and expensive "ordinary" process, however. Louisiana law meets creditors half-way with a special summary procedure called "executory process." The intricate requirements and details of executory process are beyond the scope of this book (*see* §9-629; C. Civ. P. arts. 2631–44), but the general outline is as follows: Without citation or service on the debtor, the creditor submits to the court a petition requesting seizure and sale of the collateral by the sheriff. The petition must be accompanied by documents evidencing the debt, along with the security agreement (which must include a confession of judgment by the debtor). The court will then issue a writ of seizure and sale, pursuant to which the local sheriff will both repossess the collateral and sell it at a public auction. Note that the sheriff will not seize the collateral and turn it over to the creditor; a public auction of the collateral is required. Executory process is slower and more costly than self-help repossession (as the sheriff's fees for seizure and auction have priority over the creditor's claim), but it is in many ways superior to the full-blown ordinary process of service and citation, suing on the debt, and obtaining a judgment after long pre-trial (or pre-default judgment) delays.

Since January 1, 2005, one class of creditors has been authorized to engage in self-help repossession of one type of collateral in Louisiana. Under the new "Additional Default Remedies Act," chartered financial institutions, licensed consumer credit lenders, and licensed motor vehicle sales lenders can engage in largely the same "self-help repossession" allowed outside Louisiana, but only with respect to "motor vehicles." Such self help is subject to a "breach of the peace" restriction (with definitions of what constitutes a breach) and a number of documentary and notice requirements (including a definition of "default" as two consecutive missed payments), and any individual carrying out the actual repossession process must be specially licensed to do so. For the details of this highly regulated process, see La. Rev. Stat. 6:965–67.

(c) Redemption or Foreclosure

Repossessing the collateral is only half the battle, as the debtor retains the right to buy back, or "redeem," repossessed collateral by paying off the secured debt plus the creditor's reasonable repossession expenses. §9-623. This right of redemption can be cut off, or "foreclosed," only by one of the three acts identified in the law: (1) collection of third-party obligations (*see above*, §9(b)), (2) auction or other disposition of the collateral by the sheriff or the creditor, or (3) a "strict foreclosure" collateral-for-debt exchange. §9-623(c). The latter two methods of "foreclosure" are discussed here.

(1) Judicial Disposition

Because self-help repossession is generally forbidden in Louisiana, and because the writ issued to the sheriff is one for seizure *and sale*, the debtor's redemption right is probably most often "foreclosed" through a public auction of the collateral. The process and requirements of "sheriff's sales" are carefully regulated by other law and will not be discussed here. From the creditor's (and debtor's) perspective, two points deserve a brief mention.

First, the secured creditor can bid at the sheriff's auction in "credit" dollars, and many public auctions result in the creditor's "buying" the collateral in exchange for covering the sheriff's fees and applying the "credit bid" to the debtor's unpaid obligation. Second, to the extent the auction proceeds do not cover the sheriff's fees and the secured creditor's claims, a "deficiency" remains, which can be enforced against the debtor (unless otherwise provided by contract). §9-615(d)(2). The deficiency will likely be unsecured, so it may be enforced only through ordinary process and levy on the debtor's other available property (if any).

(2) Creditor Disposition

If the collateral is in the creditor's possession (e.g., because the security interest was "possessory," or the debtor surrendered or abandoned the collateral or consented after default to its repossession by the creditor), the creditor can dispose of it—that is, realize its value by sale or otherwise. Sale is not the only option, although it is probably the most common method of creditor disposition of collateral. The sale (or other disposition, such as leasing or licensing) may be effected through public or private auction, the timing and terms of which are completely at the creditor's discretion. The primary limitation on the creditor's discretion here is that every aspect of the disposition must be "commercially reasonable." §9-610(b). This vague standard offers little guidance, although since 2001, Article 9 establishes a few guidelines for what clearly is commercially reasonable (and what clearly is not unreasonable). Just because a higher price could have been produced by a different method of disposition does not render the chosen disposition unreasonable, but beyond that, there are few clear directions. §9-627.

Just like in a judicial public auction, the creditor can bid for the collateral at a non-judicial public auction. If the creditor conducts a *private* sale, however, the creditor can bid at its own limited-invitation auction only if the collateral is "of a kind that is customarily sold on a recognized market or the subject of widely distributed standard price quotations." §9-610(c)(2). Thus, creditors might bid at private auction for collateral such as gold, publicly traded securities, or petroleum. Creditors *cannot* properly bid at private auctions for collateral like real estate or used cars, as such items are subject to significant individual price negotiation. §9-610 official cmt. 9.

Before disposition, the creditor must send notice to essentially anyone with an interest in the collateral, including the debtor and any other creditors with filing-perfected security interests in the collateral. §9-611. This notice isn't required if the collateral is perishable, will depreciate quickly, or is of a type customarily sold on a recognized market. Otherwise, the notice has to be sent within a "reasonable" time before disposition. As a matter of law, 10 days is sufficient before the earliest disposition in non-consumer cases, and 21 days is sufficient for consumer transactions. §9-612. Legally sufficient forms and contents for these notifications in non-consumer and consumer transactions are described in §§9-613 and 9-614. The debtor can waive this notice, but only in an authenticated agreement entered into *after default.* §9-624(a).

The proceeds of the creditor's disposition must be applied first to the costs of preparation and sale, then to the creditor's secured obligation, and finally to any subordinate secured obligations (if the secured party receives timely notice from such other secured parties). §9-615(a). Any excess must be turned over to the debtor (not to creditors with unsecured claims who might demand payment), though most dispositions conclude with a deficiency still owing to the secured creditor. §9-615(d). In consumer transactions, if the creditor seeks to collect the remaining deficiency from the debtor, it must send to the debtor a written explanation of how the deficiency was calculated. §9-616.

Although the creditor might be subject to actual or statutory damages for certain failures to comply with these enforcement procedures, generally a non-complying creditor will simply lose the right to collect on any remaining deficiency. §9-625. If the debtor challenges the enforcement procedures (most likely in a responsive pleading to the creditor's demand for payment of the deficiency), the creditor bears the burden of proving that it complied with Article 9 (e.g., that it acted "commercially reasonably"). §9-626(a)(1)–(2). If the creditor fails to establish its compliance with the law, it loses the difference between the actual proceeds of the disposition and the amount a complying disposition would have produced. In Louisiana, in a consumer transaction, that amount is presumably the entire deficiency (the creditor bears the burden of rebutting this presumption). §9-626(a)(4). In non-consumer transactions, no presumption applies, and the debtor bears the burden of showing how much more a proper sale would have produced. §9-626(a)(3)(B).

(3) "Strict" Foreclosure (*Dation en Paiement*)

In some cases, the creditor might prefer simply to retain the collateral as satisfaction of part or all of the secured debt. This collateral-for-debt exchange process is often called "strict foreclosure." It is the equivalent of the civil law act of "giving in payment" (*dation en paiement*), though Article 9, rather than the Civil Code, governs the "giving in payment" of collateral subject to a security interest.

The creditor initiates a "strict" foreclosure by sending a proposal to the debtor, any creditors with filing-perfected security interests in the collateral, and any other persons who notify the creditor of their interests in the collateral. §§9-620, 9-621. If the creditor proposes to retain the collateral in *partial* satisfaction of the secured debt, the debtor can accept the proposal only by agreeing to the terms of the proposal in a post-default authenticated record. §9-620(c)(1). In consumer transactions, proposals for and acceptances of partial satisfaction must contain several clear statements regarding the remaining deficiency. *See* §9-620(h)–(i). If the creditor proposes to retain the collateral in *full* satisfaction of the secured debt, the debtor can accept by authenticated record, but the debtor is *presumed* to accept unconditional proposals for full satisfaction unless the debtor sends and the creditor receives an authenticated record objecting to the proposal within 20 days after the proposal is sent. §9-620(c)(2). In addition, parties with interests in the collateral can prevent strict foreclosure by objecting within 20 days of the creditor's sending any proposal. §9-620(a)(2), (d).

In most cases, strict foreclosure requires no intermediate step of re-possession of the collateral. If the debtor accepts the strict foreclosure proposal, presumably acceptance implies that the debtor will turn over the collateral to the creditor. If the collateral is consumer goods, how-ever, the collateral cannot be in the possession of the debtor when the debtor accepts a strict foreclosure proposal. §9-620(a)(3). In addition, if the debtor has paid 60% of the principal obligation secured by con-sumer goods, no strict foreclosure (partial or full) is allowed at all un-less the debtor waives mandatory disposition in a post-default au-thenticated record. §§9-620(a)(4), (e), 9-624(c).

Chapter 2

Mortgages in Immovable Property

§ 10 Introduction, Establishment of Mortgages

(a) Introduction

Up to this point, we have focused on law that is generally uniform throughout the United States—each state has enacted Article 9 of the UCC into its commercial law in more or less the same form (although recall that Louisiana's version differs substantially from the standard version from time to time). If the collateral is not movable property, but instead *immovable* property and related rights (such as ownership or lease interests in land, usufructs, servitudes, etc.), the law governing secured transactions involving such collateral is called "mortgage" law, and it differs more substantially from state to state. The rules are quite similar around the nation, but the location of those rules in the body of the law and especially the terminology used to describe such rules varies from region to region. Luckily for us, in Louisiana, the law of mortgage is concentrated in its own part of the Civil Code, with some specific details covered in the Code Ancillaries in Title 9 of the Revised Statutes.

The range of issues that arise in this area of the law is much narrower than with respect to movable collateral, as land does not cross state lines or produce separate proceeds that are also governed by mortgage law. The rules here are designed to be clear and simple to provide maximum clarity and predictability in transactions involving sometimes very large secured loans. Since 1993, this law has been streamlined even further, making the job of planners much easier. Because secured transactions involving immovable property often stretch over many years, though, one must be familiar with the law that governed when the transaction arose, and so some familiarity with historical developments is crucial in this area. This chapter will discuss the history and current state of mortgage law in Louisiana.

(b) Conventional Mortgages

The rules for "establishing" a mortgage by contract, effective against the property owner (here called the "mortgagor," see below), are quite similar to the rules for attachment of a consensual security interest in movable property. Most conventional mortgages are memorialized in a document called an "Act of Mortgage," and all must meet four requirements. The mortgage must 1) be in a written contract, 2) be signed by the mortgagor, 3) state the amount secured or the maximum secured amount that may be outstanding at any given time, and 4) describe "precisely the nature and situation" of the immovable property affected. Civ. C. arts. 3287–88.

(1) Written Contract

The word "convention" is simply another way of saying "agreement" or "contract," so a conventional mortgage arises by contract, subject to a simple form requirement. The contract must be in writing. The Uniform Electronic Transactions Act, as adopted by Louisiana, La. Rev. Stat. 9:2601 *et seq.*, theoretically allows for the substitution of electronic records for the paper-and-ink writing historically required here, but most parties will continue to fulfill this requirement by memorializing their mortgage contracts on paper.

(2) Signed by the Mortgagor

Only the property owner—the person conveying contingent property rights—needs to sign the contract, as the evidentiary and cautionary functions of signed writings apply only to that person (evidencing the conveyance of mortgage rights in that person's property, and cautioning him or her as to the scope of rights being transferred away). No witnesses or notary signatures are required to form a valid conventional mortgage, although there are certain advantages to memorializing a mortgage in an "authentic act" (signed by two witnesses before a notary who also signs, Civ. C. art. 1833). For example, an authentic act is "self-proving" (i.e., more readily admissible as evidence in court), and a mortgage in authentic form can be enforced through the simpler and quicker method of "executory process." Mortgages under private signature alone are enforceable against the property owner, but in case of dispute, their genuineness might have to be proven by extrinsic evidence, and they must be enforced by cumbersome "ordinary" process.

Note carefully the terminology here. The person conveying rights in property (e.g., the homeowner) is called the "mortgagor," while the person receiving the contingent power to seize such rights upon default of the principal obligation (e.g., the bank) is called the "mortgagee." The mortgagor generally is but need not be also the obligor on the secured obligation. One can grant a mortgage in one's property to secure payment or performance of someone *else*'s obligation. Just like the term "debtor" in Article 9 of the UCC, the term "mortgagor" refers to the owner of the immovable property (or property rights) subject to the mortgage—*not* necessarily to the person who owes the secured debt. For example, my mother might grant a mortgage on her home to secure repayment of a loan to me (and if I default on my obligation, the mortgagee might take my mother's house, even if she had nothing otherwise to do with my loan). In such a case, generally only the mortgaged property, not the mortgagor, is bound to fulfill the principal obligation, and the law specifically affirms this arrangement. Civ. C. art. 3297. Such a mortgage, enforceable only against the property but not against the property owner, is often called an "in rem" or "non-recourse" mortgage.

(3) State the Amount Secured

Most mortgages simply state that they secure a certain amount borrowed by the property owner, plus accruing interest. The total secured amount, or at least its calculation, is clear and fixed. But sometimes businesses, for example, want to use immovable property to secure fluctuating lines of credit, in which the total amount borrowed and outstanding at any given moment rises and falls as the business "draws" on the line of credit and repays portions of it over time. From the business's perspective, this piecemeal, give-and-take approach is preferable to taking a large loan immediately and paying interest on amounts that the business does not necessarily need right away. For reasons discussed below (*see below* § 13), using a mortgage on immovable property to secure such "floating" indebtedness obligations was quite complicated until 1993, but a reform of the law in that year made things much simpler. Now, a mortgage may either state an exact, fixed amount to be secured by the mortgage (perhaps plus accruing interest), or it can state the maximum amount of a floating debt that can be outstanding at any one time secured by the mortgage.

Incidentally, although a loan or series of loans is in most cases the secured principal obligation, *any* lawful obligation can be secured by a mortgage. Civ. C. art. 3293. If performance of a non-monetary obligation is secured, though, the mortgage must state a dollar figure that represents the parties' agreement as to the maximum amount of *damages* for breach of that obligation that will be secured by the mortgage. Civ. C. art. 3294. For example, the mortgagor might grant a mortgage in her home to secure her faithful performance of a contract for services, in which case the mortgage would have to state a dollar figure and explain that it represents the maximum amount of damages for failure to perform the services called for in the contract. The collateral property will serve as security for the lesser of the amount of any judgment for damages for breach of the contract, or the amount stated in the mortgage (if the damages award exceeds that amount).

(4) Describe the Mortgaged Property

Perhaps the most important aspect of the mortgage document is the description of the property serving as collateral. Unlike the quite liberal rules for describing movable collateral in a security agreement, immovable collateral must be described with a rather high level of specificity in a mortgage. The requirements for the amount of specificity demanded of the description of the mortgaged property developed in the courts over a long period of time, and the codification of this requirement in the Civil Code "is intended to insure that this jurisprudence will continue to be authoritative in determining what kinds of descriptions are sufficient." Civ. C. art. 3288, cmt. (b). Some older decisions accepted rather relaxed descriptions of property, but the recent jurisprudential trend is generally to demand more accuracy and specificity.

Today, careful lawyers use the complex "legal description" of property, described by "metes and bounds" or more commonly, by the tract system established in the 19th century. Such descriptions refer, e.g., to parcels bounded by lines so many feet from the "northeast quarter" of a numbered "section" of a "township" and "range." Alternatively, and quite commonly, documents of sale and mortgage describe the property by reference to subdivision and plat maps on public file. Simple reference to the property's municipal address most likely will not satisfy the description requirement, and this is decidedly not the best practice even in an emergency situation. Good practice calls for careful review of the legal description of the property in recent sale documents or perhaps the public register maintained by local authorities.

Remember that rights short of absolute ownership may also be mortgaged, such as the lessee's temporary rights of use and occupancy of immovable property subject to a lease. In this case, the mortgage might describe the mortgaged property (actually, only a limited property right) by describing the lease itself by reference to a filing number in the conveyance records, or it might set forth a legal description of the property and the nature of the lessee's rights in that property in detail. Note that the lessor's (landlord's) ownership interest in the property may be mortgaged just like any other ownership right, but the right to collect the stream of rental payments is subject to special rules. Although the rent and the right to collect it are "movables," Article 9 of the UCC does not govern interests in rents on immovable property. La. Rev. Stat. 10:9-109(d)(11). The regime governing the assignment (including contingent assignment as security) of rents on immovable property are largely the same as for mortgages, and such an assignment can be effected in an Act of Mortgage. La. Rev. Stat. 9:4401. We will not review that statute in detail here, but be aware that it sets up a parallel system for rents on immovables.

Unlike Article 9 for security interests in future movables, mortgage law does not allow for the encumbrance of indefinite "after-acquired" immovable property. Some future rights in immovables may be mortgaged, though. First, as a matter of law, a mortgage encompasses not only the described property, but also all component parts affixed to that property at any point, including in the future. Civ. C. arts. 469, 3286 cmt (b), and 3291; La. Rev. Stat. 9:5391. Second, one can mortgage *specific* property that the mortgagor does not yet own but expects to acquire in the future. So long as a detailed description of the property is provided, the mortgage will be "established" in that described property when the mortgagor acquires rights in it. Civ. C. art. 3292. Thus, general future property may not be mortgaged ("all of my immovable property, presently owned or after-acquired"), but specific property that might be acquired in the future may be mortgaged in the present, so long as the property is sufficiently described in the mortgage.

(c) Legal and Judicial Mortgages

Whereas a conventional mortgage is created by contract with the property owner, two other types of mortgage are far less complicated, because they involve no agreement and no complicated terms and limitations. "Legal" and "judicial" mortgages arise as a matter of law on the terms and under the circumstances specified in the law, not as provided for in a mortgage contract.

(1) Special v. General Mortgages

Conventional mortgages are "special" mortgages, which means they encumber only the specific property described in the mortgage document. Civ. C. art. 3285. Legal and judicial mortgages, in contrast, are "general" mortgages; that is, they encumber *all* of the mortgagor's immovable property, present and future, within certain geographical limits. Civ. C. art. 3302–03.

(2) Legal Mortgages

A legal mortgage arises whenever a specific law provides for it. For example, a natural tutor must obtain a certificate stating the value of all of the child-tutee's property, and this certificate must be filed in the mortgage records of all parishes where the tutor owns immovable property. When this is accomplished, a legal mortgage is established over all of the tutor's immovable property in favor of the child-tutee to secure the value of all of the child's property. C. Civ. P. art. 4134. Such "legal" mortgages are relatively rare, so we will not dwell on them further here.

(3) Judicial Mortgages

A judicial mortgage arises when a judgment creditor on a money judgment (but not for other, non-monetary judgments) files a certified copy of the judgment in the mortgage records of a parish in which the judgment debtor has immovable property. Civ. C. arts. 3299–3300. This mortgage secures the judgment debtor's payment of the amount specified in the judgment; that is, if the judgment debtor does not pay, the judgment creditor-mortgagee can have the debtor's immovable property seized and sold (in preference to other creditors) to satisfy the judgment. A suspensive appeal of the money judgment has no effect on the judicial mortgage thus created. Civ. C. art. 3304. A money judgment prescribes 10 years after it is rendered, Civ. C. art. 3501, so to preserve the judicial mortgage securing the judgment, it must be "revived" in a simple proceeding filed before expiration, C. Civ. P. art. 2031, *in addition to* the mortgage's being "reinscribed" every 10 years according to the rules discussed below (*see below* § 11(b); Civ. C. arts. 3359, 3362).

(d) Mortgages Without a Mortgage: Pignorative Contracts & Bonds for Deed

Sometimes, creditors wish to avoid the requirements of mortgage law but nonetheless to obtain the advantages of using property to secure performance of an obligation. A long line of *jurisprudence constante*, however, establishes that a transaction that is "in the nature of a secured transaction" will be treated as one, even if it is called or documented otherwise by the parties. For example, in the 19th century, lenders would issue loans to borrowers ostensibly as payment for a "sale" of items of the borrowers' property to the lenders "subject to a right of redemption." In such sham "sales," the borrower would remain in possession of the property, and if the borrower paid back the secret loan, that fulfilled the "redemption" condition, and ownership would transfer back to the borrower. If the borrower failed to repay the loan, however, the lender already "owned" the property and could therefore ask the sheriff to repossess the property, which the lender would resell to cover the unpaid loan after the redemption period had expired. Clever lawyers dreamed up such transactions to allow creditors to avoid the cost and inconvenience of observing the requirements and restrictions (including protections for borrowers) of security device law.

Such disguised secured transactions are called "pignorative" contracts, from the Latin *"pignus"* and *"pignoratio"* —handing something over as security in pledge. If a transaction is found to be pignorative, it will be recharacterized as a secured transaction, and if the requirements of a secured transaction have not been met (e.g., the form requirements for a conventional mortgage), the "secured creditor" might lose the protections it illegitimately sought. Continuing with the above example, if the "sale subject to redemption" transaction is deemed pignorative, the court might nullify the sale as against public policy and refuse to allow the lender to repossess the property from the defaulting borrower. *See, e.g.,* Civ. C. art. 2569; *Guste v. Hibernia Nat'l Bank,* 655 So.2d 724, 732 (La. 4th Cir. 1995).

There is one notable exception to this rule prohibiting pignorative transactions. In a "bond for deed" transaction, the seller of an immovable remains the legal owner of the property but transfers possession to a buyer in exchange for the buyer's promise to pay the purchase price over time (and the seller generally promises to apply the buyer's payments to the seller's unpaid mortgage note). The deal is that the seller will transfer the "deed" (ownership of the property) only when the borrower has fulfilled his "bond" (promise to pay the purchase price of the property). Such transactions are attractive, for example, when mortgage interest rates are high, and the current owner of an immovable has a low-interest mortgage loan. The buyer might prefer to pay off the seller's low-interest installment loan, plus some profit to the seller, rather than financing the entire purchase with a higher-interest new loan.

This is a very dangerous situation for the buyer. Without some special legal regulation, the seller could immediately repossess the property (which she still owns) if the buyer fails to make any payment, and the buyer might have to sue for a refund of any amounts already paid. Moreover, even if the buyer does pay, if the seller fails to apply the buyer's payments to the seller's unpaid low-interest mortgage note, the seller's bank's mortgage will continue to encumber the property even after the buyer has paid the entire contract price to the seller. To receive a clean "deed," the buyer will have to pay to the seller's bank whatever the seller failed to remit to the mortgage lender. Louisiana has a special law protecting buyers in "bond for deed" contracts. La. Rev. Stat. 9:2941–48. The details of this statute are beyond the scope of this book, but again, be aware that this relatively common transaction is governed by special law, which is the only reason this pignorative contract is supported by law. Incidentally, banks dislike bond-for-deed sales, because they allow buyers essentially to cheat the banks out of more interest on new loans. Thus, banks generally include "due on sale" clauses in mortgage notes (and the law imposes such clauses on certain mortgage notes, La. Rev. Stat. 6:833). The effect of such a clause is to allow the bank to "accelerate" (make immediately payable in full) the entire amount owed on the mortgage note upon any sale of the property. A buyer thus cannot continue to pay the seller's installments, as they are all due immediately, so the buyer must obtain a new loan for the entire purchase price.

§ 11 "Perfection" of Mortgages: Filing and Recordation

As discussed above in the context of movable collateral (*see above* § 3), establishing rights enforceable against the property owner is only part of the battle—and often not the most important part. To make a mortgage effective against *third parties* who might also establish rights in the collateral (e.g., later buyers of the property or other creditors who might establish mortgages in the same property), the mortgagee must provide notice to such third parties of the existence of the mortgagee's rights. With respect to Article 9 security interests in movable collateral, recall that this process is called "perfection" and is generally (though not always) accomplished by filing a simple notice document (the UCC-1 financing statement) in the UCC records of any parish clerk of court's office. *See above* § 3.

(a) Filing for Recordation

With respect to mortgages in immovable property, in contrast, the process is called "registry" or "recordation," and the original mortgage document itself must be filed in the mortgage records of the parish in which the immovable property is located. Civ. C. arts. 3341, 3346. Filing a mortgage in the proper office is the *only* way to make the mortgage effective against third parties. In the "olden days," the clerk would actually "record" the text of each filed mortgage in the central register by hand. This process often occupied quite some time after filing, and the mortgage in some cases was technically effective only after it had been recorded. Today, simply *filing* the mortgage with the proper recorder of mortgages produces as a matter of law the "effect of recordation." Civ. C. art. 3347. The moment of effectiveness is established when the recorder stamps the document with the date and time of filing. Civ. C. art. 3348.

For historical reasons, unlike many other states, Louisiana's immovable property records are divided into two separate sets: The conveyance records hold acts of sale, lease, and donation of immovables, and the mortgage records collect acts of mortgage and privilege over immovables. Civ. C. arts. 3338, 3346. In all parishes, the clerk of the district court maintains both of these two sets of records. La. Rev. Stat. 44:71. A mortgage *must* be filed in the proper records to be effective. By the way, to save on filing fees, extracts (after July 1, 2006, called "notices") of leases may be filed in the conveyance records, La. Rev. Stat. 44:112, but extracts are not acceptable for mortgages. The entire original act of mortgage (or a certified copy of an original recorded in another parish, Civ. C. art. 3355) must be filed in the mortgage records. Civ. C. arts. 3338, 3344–45 (allowing recordation of copies rather than originals after July 1, 2006).

Once again, the act of mortgage need not be in authentic form (signed before two witnesses and notarized) to be recorded, but an authentic act offers certain important advantages. *See above* § 10(b)(2). Present law has also done away with a previous formality with respect to the secured note, which now need not be marked in any special way. Before 1993, the notary was required to place a "paraph" on a note secured by a mortgage to show that the note and mortgage were connected. The paraph was a simple statement on the note, like the following:

"NE VARIETUR"

For identification with an act of mortgage passed before me this [day] day of [month], [year] at Baton Rouge, LA.

/s/ NOTARY PUBLIC

The "ne varietur" is Latin for "let it not be changed," and the paraph simply ensured that it would be clear exactly which obligation was secured by the mortgage. Although the parties can ask that a note be paraphed in this way for clarity, this is not necessary any more (even for executory process, La. Rev. Stat. 9:5555). Civ. C. arts. 3325 and 3298(C).

In a minority of states, the law says that an unfiled mortgage can be effective against third parties if they have *notice* that the mortgage exists. Such states are said to have "notice statutes." In Louisiana and most other states, acts affecting immovables, including mortgages, are effective against third parties only from the moment of filing in the proper office, regardless of any notice or knowledge on the part of third parties. Louisiana and other such states are said to have "pure race" statutes. The first person to win the "race" to the courthouse and record his or her rights in the proper office wins.

The simple fact of having placed the mortgage in the public records is the key, but the only way a mortgage can fulfill its notice function is if third parties can find it by searching the index of grantors and grantees by the mortgagor's name. Unlike the Article 9 rules for the debtor's name on the UCC-1, however, mortgage law contains little guidance on how accurate the mortgagor's name must be. Effective July 1, 2006, a new rule provides that a filed mortgage document is effective even if it contains an erroneous or inaccurate mortgagor's name so long as the name listed "is not so indefinite, incomplete, or erroneous as to be misleading and the instrument as a whole reasonably alerts a person examining the records that the instrument may be that of the party." Civ. C. art. 3353. This vague provision will require judicial interpretation and application before anything clear can be said about just how accurate the mortgagor's name must be. Good practice, of course, is to use the complete and accurate legal name of the debtor, consistent with similar practice under UCC Article 9. *See above* § 3(a).

(b) Lapse and Reinscription

Filing is not forever. To be effective against third parties, a mortgage must have been properly filed *and* the effectiveness of its inscription in the mortgage records must not have lapsed. Just like the UCC records for Article 9 security interests, *see above* § 7(d), the mortgage records are "self purging," so old mortgages are automatically invalidated against third parties after a certain time.

The effective period of a filed mortgage is indicated by applying two rules. First, the default rule is that a mortgage is effective on the records for 10 years after the date of the mortgage document (when it was executed). Civ. C. art. 3357. The second rule is an exception to the first rule, although it probably applies more often. If the mortgage document describes the maturity date (due date) of the secured obligation, and any part of that obligation matures 9 years or later after the date of the mortgage document, such a mortgage is effective for 6 more years after the latest maturity date of the described obligation. Civ. C. art. 3358. For example, most home mortgages recite that they secure home loans payable in installments over very long periods, most often 15 or 30 years. Such a mortgage is effective on the records for 21 or 36 years, respectively; that is, 15 or 30 years (the latest maturity date of any part of the described secured obligation) plus 6 more years. To understand these rules fully, put yourself in the position of a searcher. Only if you can tell by looking at a filed mortgage document that the obligation secured comes due 9 years or longer after the date you see on the mortgage document, then inscription lapses 6 years after that date; otherwise, it lapses 10 years after the date you see on the act of mortgage.

One more wrinkle allows shorter-term mortgages to be effective for longer than 10 years. A mortgage can be amended, perhaps because of a renegotiation of the principal obligation or the repayment term. If a filed amendment satisfies the requirements of the exceptional rule (i.e., it describes a new maturity date of any part of the obligation that is 9 years or later after the date of the original act of mortgage), then inscription will be effective for 6 years after the new maturity date. Civ. C. art. 3361. No other amendment affects the duration of inscription of a mortgage.

Because mortgages often secure debts lasting for 30 years or longer, we must understand that older law (former Civ. C. art. 3369, significantly revised in 1993) measured the effectiveness of a filed mortgage from the date of the *obligation*—not the date of the mortgage document—regardless of whether or not the mortgage stated the maturity date of the obligation. This rule still applies to mortgages created before January 1, 1993. Thus, a filed pre-1993 mortgage that does not state the maturity date of the obligation may nonetheless be effective on the records for more than 10 years after the date of the mortgage document. For example, a pre-1993 mortgage securing a 30-year home loan note is still effective on the records today (in 2006) even if it does not describe the maturity date of the obligation and even though more than 10 years has passed. Such a mortgage is effective on the records for 36 years after the date of the obligation.

To maintain an effectively recorded mortgage, it must be "reinscribed" before lapse. This is a simple process in which the mortgagee (creditor) signs and files a written "notice of reinscription" in the same office where the original mortgage was filed. The notice must "declare that the [mortgage] is reinscribed" and state 1) the name of the mortgagor (as stated in the originally recorded mortgage) and 2) the registry or other recordation number of the original filed mortgage (or previous notice of reinscription). Civ. C. art. 3362. This simple notice extends the mortgage for ten more years after the date of the filing of the notice (*not* from the original lapse date of the mortgage). Civ. C. art. 3364. Filing this simple notice is the only way to extend the effectiveness of a mortgage. Civ. C. art. 3363. If the notice is filed *after* the effect of recordation has lapsed, the notice functions to "revive" the lapsed mortgage inscription for 10 more years, but the priority date of the mortgage is reset to the (much later) date of filing of the late notice. Civ. C. art. 3365.

§ 12 Transfer of Mortgages and Mortgaged Property

Both mortgaged property and secured obligations are often transferred from the original mortgagor and mortgagee to third parties. Mortgage law addresses such situations to protect the rights of the original and subsequent parties. This section discusses the rules relating to transfers of the secured obligation by the mortgagee, as well as transfers of the collateral property by the mortgagor.

(a) Transfer of the Secured Principal Obligation

The first, relatively easy scenario involves the secured creditor's transfer of the principal obligation along with the mortgage. Sometimes a mortgage bank might want to "cash out" its long-term secured claim against the mortgagor and put that money to other, immediate use. In such a case, the mortgagee might sell (assign) the obligation to another bank or investor who then steps into the bank's shoes with respect to the obligation. The law clarifies that the transferee of the secured obligation automatically also steps into the original mortgagee's shoes with respect to the rights represented by the mortgage. A transfer of a principal obligation automatically carries with it a transfer of any accessory real rights, such as a mortgage. Civ. C. arts. 2645, 3312. No separate transfer or assignment of the mortgage is necessary; indeed, transferring only the mortgage would have no effect, as mortgages cannot survive separate from their principal obligations.

This rule is subject to two small twists. First, the transferee might receive *greater* rights than the original mortgagee had if a modification of the mortgage has not been recorded. Civ. C. art. 3356. Transferees take free of unrecorded modifications, so mortgagors are well advised to record any modification to the mortgage that inures to their benefit. Second, if the mortgagee transfers only part of the secured obligation(s) (e.g., one of multiple notes secured by the same mortgage), pre-1993 law suggested that the original mortgagee subordinated her rights to the transferee; i.e., in case of foreclosure, the original mortgagee-transferor would collect the collateral sale proceeds only after the new mortgagee-transferee had received payment in full. Now, the law clarifies that the original mortgagee-transferor and the new mortgagee-transferee rank equally in the proceeds of enforcement of the mortgage. Civ. C. arts. 3311, 3313. Multiple obligations secured by the same mortgage get paid from the proceeds of a collateral sale pro rata based on the secured amount each is owed (unless otherwise agreed).

(b) Transfer of the Mortgaged Property— "Third Possessors"

Just like Article 9 of the UCC with respect to movables, mortgage law provides that a mortgage follows the immovable property into the hands of a transferee unless the mortgagee explicitly releases the mortgage (of course, provided the mortgage has been properly recorded and is effective against third parties). Civ. C. art. 3280. The transferee of the mortgaged property will not be personally liable on the secured obligation, however, unless the transferee "assumes" the mortgage and obligation. Thus, a transfer of the property without a release of the mortgage produces an "in rem" mortgage, enforceable against the property but not personally against the property owner-transferee. *See above* § 10(b)(2). Someone who takes mortgaged property but is not personally liable on the secured obligation is called a "third possessor." Civ. C. art. 3315. Such third possessors have constitutional rights to receive notice of foreclosure before losing their property interests, but an extended discussion of these issues is beyond the scope of this book.

Mortgage law protects both mortgagees and third possessors, balancing their competing interests and incentives in two ways. First, since third possessors are not personally liable on the secured obligation, they might not be concerned about the condition of the property. To protect the interests of the mortgagee, the law imposes a duty on third possessors to indemnify (reimburse) the mortgagee for the third possessor's negligently or intentionally allowing harm to come to the property to the prejudice of the mortgagee. Civ. C. art. 3316.

Second, in contrast, if a responsible third possessor *improves* the mortgaged property, and the mortgagee later forecloses after default on the principal obligation, the third possessor might lose the value of the improvements to the mortgagee unfairly. Consequently, the law allows the third possessor in such cases to recover the costs of her improvements from the proceeds of the foreclosure sale, but only to the extent that these improvements increased the value of the property. Civ. C. art. 3318. Third possessors are well advised to have the property appraised both before and after making any significant improvement to the property, or at the very least to ask the appraiser after-the-fact to estimate the value of the property pre-improvement in addition to appraising the property as improved. The third possessor can recover only the positive difference between these "before and after" appraisals.

§13 Collateral Mortgages and Multiple Indebtedness Mortgages

A long historical struggle in Louisiana immovable finance law created the unique Louisiana concept of "collateral mortgages" and has finally been resolved by legislative acceptance of so-called "multiple indebtedness mortgages." This section describes the history and current status of these two special mortgage devices. The key issue here is how to use immovable property to secured indefinite, fluctuating future loans, and more importantly, how to make such a mortgage effective against third parties from the moment of filing for registry. Pre-1993 law required a rather complex resolution to this problem. Current law retains that resolution but allows a much simpler and more effective alternative.

Mortgage law was originally designed to deal with the most common type of transaction: the mortgagor borrows one sum (probably the purchase price of the mortgaged property), and the mortgage describes exactly that debt and secures only that obligation (plus, perhaps, interest and attorney's fees). The average home loan mortgage is of this type. The borrower can borrow more money in the future secured by the same house (e.g., a "home equity loan"), but to do so, the borrower will have to grant a new mortgage to the lender at that time, and that lender's priority in the proceeds of a foreclosure sale of the house will rank against other claimants only from the much later date on which it records that second mortgage. For reasons discussed in § 14 below, a later ranking date is not an optimal situation from the lender's perspective.

(a) Construction Mortgages: Unproblematic Future Loans

Note that the problem is *not* that mortgages cannot secure future loans. Construction mortgages, for example, have always secured loans made in the future, and this has never been a problem. In a construction project, because the building has not been built yet, banks are understandably hesitant to lend hundreds of thousands (perhaps millions) of dollars right away and trust that the builder will build a building the value of which will adequately secure the entire loan. Banks commonly protect themselves in such situations by paying out construction loans in installments (commonly called "tranches," from the French for "slice"). The mortgage document, however, describes the secured debt as the total projected amount of the construction loan. The property owner grants a mortgage on the land and projected building immediately, and although the loan will be made in installments in the future, the mortgage describes and secures the total amount that the builder projects needing to complete construction.

The loan agreement might say, for example, that the bank will lend $10,000 to complete the survey and foundation work, then a bank-hired inspector will check the work and approve the next "tranche" of the loan, say, $20,000 for the framing work. Then, when the framing is done, a bank inspector will come out and approve the framing work and release the next tranche of, say, $50,000 for exterior finishing (roofing, exterior walls and bricking, windows). Loan disbursements continue like this in "tranches" over time until the bank is satisfied that a good building secures the loan. The bank generally holds back the final "tranche" until after the bank inspector gives final approval to the building. Thus, the original mortgage, given and recorded perhaps months or years before, secures all of these future tranche loans, and the bank's priority dates from the original recording of the mortgage against anyone who gets a lien on the property. This type of mortgage to secure future loans has never been a problem, because *one* clear amount is lent out, and the mortgage secures only that amount to be paid back *once.*

(b) The Problem: Fluctuating Lines of Credit

The situation becomes more complicated when the borrower and bank are not quite sure how much money the borrower will borrow in the future (and therefore what amount of indebtedness will be secured by—and must be stated in—the mortgage). Many commercial borrowers, for example, prefer to establish a fluctuating "line of credit" to provide operating capital as needed. In a line of credit arrangement, the bank agrees to make funds available to the borrower from time to time, and to accept repayment of those funds (to avoid accruing interest) from time to time, with fewer administrative hurdles, so long as the total outstanding amount of the loan never exceeds a certain amount. The total amount outstanding rises and falls as the borrower takes more "draws" against the line of credit and repays whatever amounts it can repay along the way to avoid accruing interest on outstanding amounts. From the borrower's perspective, a line of credit is superior to the alternative of borrowing one large sum, paying interest on all of that money before it is all needed, and seeking a new loan (through the sometimes long and arduous application process) once that original loan is exhausted. Taking the loan in installments would avoid part of these problems, but the main problem remains that the total amount needed is unclear at the outset, and it will fluctuate as the borrower pays back loans and takes more "draws" from the available line over time.

The problem from the perspective of mortgage law was that, prior to 1993, mortgages could not by themselves secure *indefinite, fluctuating* amounts of future indebtedness. Judicial construction of mortgage and obligations law held that payments on loans reduced the amount secured by a mortgage automatically and irreversibly, and the mortgage was reduced (extinguished) as the borrower paid back earlier loans. Once the amount stated in the mortgage had been lent and repaid *once*, the mortgage could not secure any more loans, and a new mortgage (and a new filing and priority date) were required to secure any additional future advances.

For example, suppose Borrower entered into a line of credit agreement with Bank, making available a maximum amount of $5 million outstanding at any given time, secured by a mortgage on Borrower's immovable property. Suppose further that Borrower had "drawn" $2 million in loans on the line of credit in year one, $2 million in year two, and $1 million in year three, maxing out the $5 million available under the line of credit at any one time. In year four, Borrower's business started to boom, so it began repaying the outstanding loans. It repaid $2 million in the first few months of year 4, making $2 million available for more future loans on the line of credit again. But by the end of year 4, Borrower needed more money, so it took an additional $500,000 loan. The problem was that pre-1993 mortgage law held that repayment of the $2 million in year 4 *extinguished* the original secured obligation by that amount, and the mortgage with it. Once the entire amount described in the mortgage had been lent out *once*, the original mortgage simply could not secure any more future loans under the line of credit. A new mortgage with a new filing and ranking date was required for later loans, such as the $500,000 draw taken late in year 4. This is a classic example of law undermining rather than facilitating accepted commercial practice—perhaps for good reason, such as protecting intervening claimants or the borrower, but fluctuating line of credit borrowing was severely hindered.

(c) Temporary Fix #1: The Collateral Mortgage Package

Already in the 1800s, brilliant and creative Louisiana lawyers found a way around this problem by combining a different, more flexible security device with the more rigidly regulated mortgage. These highly skilled lawyers understood all of security device law, and they realized that the law governing security interests in *movable* collateral freely allowed for securing fluctuating lines of credit.

Recall that a security interest in a movable under Article 9 of the UCC can (and often does) secure any and all indebtedness of whatever kind or source whenever arising, in the past, present, or future, and the security agreement need not describe the debt in any particular detail. *See above* § 2(c)(2). The pre-1990 predecessor to Article 9 of the UCC in Louisiana law was a series of articles in the Civil Code on "pledge." Civ. C. arts. 3133–53 (superseded by UCC Article 9, as adopted in Louisiana, effective January 1, 1990). The word "pledge" is still used today to describe the somewhat rare secured transaction in which the creditor takes possession of movable collateral. *See above* § 2(c)(1). Under the former law of pledge, just like under current UCC Article 9, a security interest in movable property *could* secure fluctuating future loans of any kind, with no need to describe in writing the exact amount secured (indeed, under former and current law, no writing at all is required with respect to oral agreements to turn over property to the creditor in pledge). *See above* § 2(c)(1).

The question was how to combine the flexibility of movable security device law (pledge) with the value of a security device in immovable property (mortgage). Through a stunningly creative bit of legal maneuvering, clever Louisiana lawyers constructed a new transaction centered around a fictitious promissory note, which could be pledged, and which was in turn secured by a mortgage on immovable property. The note and the mortgage thus served as "collateral" for the *real* principal obligation(s), so all of the documents in this transaction came to be called collectively a "collateral mortgage" package, or just a "collateral mortgage."

(1) Pledge of the Collateral Mortgage Note
("Ne Varietur" Note)

To create the center of the transaction, the borrower would sign a promissory note, called a "collateral mortgage note." This note was generally payable upon demand, generally "to bearer," but sometimes to the borrower herself, for the full amount of the line of credit maximum, plus some cushion for extra charges and expenses (for a total of generally 150% of the maximum available under the line of credit). That note thus represented an immediately valuable movable. Anyone in possession of this demand bearer note (or becoming a holder of an order note) theoretically had the right to collect the full face amount of the note upon demand at any time. This valuable note could be pledged (negotiated to the lender) as security for any and all indebtedness that the borrower would at any point owe to the lender, including whatever fluctuating indebtedness borrower might incur over time as the line of credit was drawn and repaid.

Generally, a written "collateral pledge agreement" evidenced the terms of this pledge arrangement, but passage of possession of the collateral mortgage note to the lender (along with oral testimony regarding the debt secured) was before and is today sufficient evidence. Civ. C. art. 3158(B); La. Rev. Stat. 10:9-203(b)(3)(B). Under pledge law (and today under UCC Article 9), the lender would always have priority in the collateral mortgage note against any third party creditor, as to both current and future loans, so long as the lender retained possession of the note. La. Rev. Stat. 10:9-330(d); 9:5551(B). The collateral mortgage note was previously required to be paraphed "ne varietur" for identification with the collateral mortgage (*see above* § 11(a) *and below* § 13(c)(3)), so the collateral mortgage note was often also called the "ne varietur note."

(2) Hand Note(s)

Everyone understood that the borrower did not *really* promise to pay 150% of the maximum amount available under the line of credit to anyone who presented the collateral mortgage note for payment at any time. The collateral mortgage note had only *theoretical* value and was a *fictional* device that served only to anchor the collateral mortgage transaction. This "common knowledge" offered cold comfort to wary out-of-state borrowers signing such notes, but the Louisiana Supreme Court in 2001 finally established that this custom represented the law. *Diamond Services Corp. v. Benoit*, 780 So.2d 367 (La. 2001). The borrower *really* agreed to repay only actual loans made (draws taken) under the line of credit. These real loans were generally but not necessarily represented by other, real promissory notes, often called "hand notes." The "hand notes" and any other loans from lender to borrower represented the real principal obligation fictionally secured by the collateral mortgage note.

(3) The Collateral Mortgage

If the "real" obligation was represented by the hand notes, the "real" security device was a mortgage, called the "collateral mortgage," that encumbered the very real value of the described immovable property. Not only did the collateral mortgage note represent a valuable movable that could be pledged to secure the hand note(s), it also represented an obligation that could itself be secured by a mortgage. So instead of securing the indefinite future hand notes with a mortgage (which mortgage law hindered, as discussed above), the lender would secure the collateral mortgage note with a mortgage. The collateral mortgage note represented an obligation—albeit a fictional one—with a clear and present amount that would not change over time, so a simple mortgage could easily secure that amount. The borrower granted the collateral mortgage in the borrower's immovable property at the same time as she pledged the movable collateral mortgage note to the lender, and the mortgage described the secured debt as the exact amount of the collateral mortgage note.

Again, no one expected the borrower to repay the obligation represented by the collateral mortgage note if she could not repay the hand note(s), so default on the hand note(s) would lead all but automatically to foreclosure, demand, and default on the collateral mortgage note (still in the lender's possession). Once the borrower defaulted on the collateral mortgage note, the lender could move to the next step in the chain and enforce the collateral mortgage securing it, seizing and selling the mortgaged immovable property and applying the sale proceeds to whatever "real" indebtedness remained outstanding.

Here, yet another fiction was necessary. Because the collateral mortgage secured only the amount of the collateral mortgage note—not the hand note(s)—the lender could realize on the value of the immovable property only up to the amount of the collateral mortgage note. This generally produced no problems, because lenders were foresighted enough to demand that the collateral mortgage note promise 150% of the agreed maximum amount of potential "hand note" obligations. Conversely, though, since the collateral mortgage note secured the hand note(s), and the collateral mortgage note was purely a fictional obligation, a jurisprudential rule developed that restricted the lender's recovery to the total amount actually owed, which was generally less than the face amount of the collateral mortgage note. Thus, the collateral mortgage secured the *lesser* of the total "real" indebtedness under the hand note(s) or the face amount of the collateral mortgage note.

This three-part transaction solved the problem of using immovable property to secure indefinite, fluctuating future loans with a present recorded mortgage. The collateral mortgage note represented a present debt for the maximum amount that could be outstanding at any given time under the line of credit, but the line of credit "hand note" loans could be repaid and re-borrowed without reducing the amount secured by the mortgage, because the mortgage secured the fictional value of the collateral mortgage note, which was never paid off. The lender always had priority in the collateral mortgage note as long as it retained possession, and the collateral mortgage was filed long ago at the beginning of the transaction, so the lender had early priority in the mortgaged property, as well. Problem solved.

In conclusion, note well two things. First, a "collateral mortgage" is *not* a separate type of mortgage. A collateral mortgage is a basic conventional mortgage that happens to be the tail of a *collateral mortgage package*. Second, since 1993, mortgage law has solved this problem directly, and conventional mortgages can secure fluctuating lines of credit, as discussed immediately below. Nonetheless, many collateral mortgage packages still exist, and many Louisiana lawyers (and bankers) continue to create new ones because they are comfortable with previous practice (however complex), and the new law is still relatively untested. Perhaps in time the collateral mortgage package will fade into the past, but that time is not yet upon us.

(4) A Final Note on Prescription

An obligation evidenced by a note prescribes 5 years after payment is exigible (due and payable). Civ. C. art. 3498. Because the collateral mortgage note is generally a demand note, it is "exigible" immediately, so it will prescribe (and the transaction will fall to pieces) 5 years after it is executed unless prescription is somehow interrupted.

The lender could have the borrower sign an act of acknowledgment of the debt represented by the collateral mortgage note every five years to reset the prescription clock, Civ. C. art. 3464, but this formalistic exercise is fortunately not necessary. Payment on an obligation also acknowledges the debt and interrupts prescription, and the borrower generally will make payments at least once every 5 years on the hand note(s). As a matter of law, any payment on a hand note or other obligation secured by a collateral mortgage note interrupts prescription on the collateral mortgage note, as well, largely solving the problem of prescription. La. Rev. Stat. 9:5807. Note that the hand note or other obligation can never prescribe as, under the "constant acknowledgement" rule, if a pledged movable is in the secured party's possession, that constantly acknowledges and interrupts prescription on the secured debt. *Scott v. Corkern*, 91 So.2d 569 (La. 1956). Thus, the pledged collateral mortgage note constantly acknowledges and interrupts prescription on the fictitiously secured hand note(s).

(d) Permanent Fix #2: Multiple Indebtedness Mortgages

Finally, in 1992, the legislature responded to the problem directly after nearly 150 years of indirect solution by practitioners. The legislature called the collateral mortgage package "a complicated and cumbersome device," and it might well have added "dangerous." Not only is it difficult to convince out-of-state firms that signing a demand note for $5 million doesn't "really" obligate them to pay $5 million immediately (particularly if the collateral mortgage note found its way into the hands of a holder in due course), but many unanswered questions remain with respect to collateral mortgage practice. Converting to new practices might expose lawyers and lenders to new risks, but continuing to adhere to previous practice with collateral mortgages is not risk free, either.

Effective January 1, 1993, the Louisiana legislature amended the Civil Code articles on mortgage to allow conventional mortgages to secure fluctuating lines of future indebtedness. A conventional mortgage that states not a fixed secured debt, but a maximum secured amount that can be outstanding at any given time, *see above*

§ 10(b)(3), is technically called a "multiple indebtedness mortgage" or a "multiple obligations mortgage." *See* La. Rev. Stat. 9:5217(B) (imposing caption, margin, and typeface requirements on such mortgages). Such mortgages now explicitly rank against third parties from the moment of their filing for registry, even if all secured loans are at some point paid off and more loans advanced later. Civ. C. art. 3298(B). Like a UCC Article 9 security agreement and financing statement, the flexible new multiple indebtedness mortgage continues to secure the borrower's fluctuating future indebtedness until all outstanding loans are repaid and the borrower requests cancellation. Civ C. art. 3298(D)–(E); La. Rev. Stat. 9:5557. Time will tell whether the courts will accept the legislature's clear and decisive abandonment of the previous restrictions of mortgage law, but the new multiple indebtedness mortgage promises a much simpler, more straightforward, and more efficient method of securing fluctuating lines of credit with mortgages in immovable property.

§ 14 Ranking Mortgages — Priorities

The law of ranking mortgage rights in immovables is similar to the law of ranking security interests in movable collateral under Article 9 of the UCC, although here, the main rule has far fewer notable exceptions: First to file wins. Whether a purchaser, lien creditor, or mortgagee claims rights in the property, the simple and steadfast rule is that claims to immovables rank in priority in ascending chronological order of the date and time of proper filing for registry of the documents evidencing their respective rights. Civ. C. arts. 3307(3), 3338, 3298(B). The same general rule applies, with an important exception for PMSIs, as between a mortgagee and a secured creditor with a fixture-filed Article 9 security interest in component parts of the immovable. *See above* § 8(d).

The only notable exception to the first-to-file rule with respect to the immovable as a whole concerns the rights of the IRS under federal tax law, which trumps state mortgage law. Even if the IRS's tax lien notice is properly filed after a mortgage, the IRS will beat the mortgagee in two respects, just as it beats prior perfected Article 9 security interests. *See above* § 8(a)(3). First, as to all property acquired by the mortgagor after the filing of the notice of tax lien, the choateness doctrine elevates the IRS's rights over any other pre-recorded rights. Second, the IRS's rights take priority over a prior filed mortgage (particularly a multiple indebtedness mortgage) to the extent that the mortgage secures advances made *either* with "actual notice or knowledge" of the IRS's notice of tax lien filing *or* after 45 days after such filing. 26 U.S.C. § 6323(d). A properly recorded mortgage will prevail over the claims of the IRS, but only in property owned by the mortgagor when the IRS files its notice, and only with respect to loans made before or perhaps very shortly after the IRS has filed its notice.

The priority rules with respect to collateral mortgage packages combine the rules for ranking Article 9 security interests and mortgages. The collateral mortgagee's priority is measured from the point at which *both* the collateral mortgage is properly filed for registry *and* the security interest (pledge) in the collateral mortgage note is perfected. La. Rev. Stat. 9:5551(A)–(B). For transactions arising before January 1, 1990, judicial construction of pledge law required only that the creditor maintain possession of the collateral mortgage note to establish perfection. After Louisiana's adoption of Article 9 of the UCC, possession is still the only way to perfect an Article 9 security interest in a collateral mortgage note, although perfection may occur in other "instruments" by filing a UCC-1 financing statement. La. Rev. Stat. 10:9-312(b)(4). Under the law both before and after 1990, if the creditor loses possession of the collateral mortgage note, priority of the collateral mortgage is reset to when possession is reestablished (and the entire transaction may crumble if the note cannot be located at all).

In addition, however, Article 9 now requires fulfillment of the three requirements for *attachment* of the security interest to the collateral mortgage note before possession by the creditor can perfect that interest. *See above* § 2. One of the requirements for attachment is that "value has been given." Thus, after 1990, collateral mortgage lenders are well advised to ensure that *some* nominal value is given contemporaneously with taking possession of the collateral mortgage note and filing of the collateral mortgage, especially if the first advance on the hand note(s) is expected only some time later. If no "value" is given at the time the lender takes possession of the collateral mortgage note, perfection of the security interest (and the ranking date for the collateral mortgage package) will not occur until value is given, most likely with the first advance under the line of credit. Note that a non-binding commitment to lend in the future under the line of credit is *not* present value for this purpose, and most lenders will be loathe to *bind* themselves to lend in the future with no discretion to refuse. *See above* § 2(a).

Chapter 3

Selected Privileges

§15 Introduction, General and Miscellaneous Special Privileges

(a) Introduction

Up to this point, we have focused on conventional real security rights—those voluntarily granted by contract by the property owner to a creditor. We nonetheless have seen two security devices that arise as a matter of law without the consent of the property owner—judicial and legal mortgages. Now we will turn to a series of security devices that *all* arise by operation of law. A statute or Code article creates such security devices and identifies both the property they affect and the claims they secure. Outside Louisiana, such security devices are generally called by the generic term "liens," or more precisely, "statutory liens." In Louisiana, such security devices have a special name: "privileges." Civ. C. arts. 3185–86. Privileges offer fewer benefits than conventional security devices, like mortgages and security interests. Privileges provide the same "reservation of rights" in property, elevating the privilege creditor's eventual claim to the affected property above the rights of competing claimants, but privileges cannot be enforced quickly and easily using executory process. Instead, privilege creditors must still sue on the unpaid obligation, obtain a judgment using ordinary process, and enforce that judgment through normal means (sheriff's levy). The privilege simply elevates the *priority* of the privilege creditor's ultimate claim to the sheriff's sale pro-

ceeds of the "collateral." As we shall see, most often the privilege creditor's rights will remain subordinate to the rights of any competing
conventionally secured creditor.

Privileges represent the legislator's attempt to encourage socially
constructive acts. The law promises that, if one confers value on
someone else through one of the identified acts (all of which indirectly benefit society), the law will enhance the actor's ability to collect payment for that value by reserving a right in identified property
of the person who benefited directly from the act. As we examine
these privileges, understand that most were enacted in the early 1800s
to encourage behavior at a very different time and under very different circumstances than those prevailing today. Many of these privilege rules are slated for revision in the near future, and one suspects
that many of these anachronistic laws will be eliminated or substantially revised. Ask yourself along the way whether these privileges
seem useful or important today, and more importantly, notice that
many of these privileges can be obtained by the "creditor" much more
effectively through a negotiated, conventional security device or
mortgage. Needless to say, we will focus on the privileges that might
have application today and downplay or ignore those that have little
or no current economic significance.

(b) General v. Special Privileges

The law creates two kinds of privileges: "general" and "special." Civ.
C. arts. 3190, 3216, 3249, 3252. General privileges extend to all of
the debtor's property. Special privileges, in contrast, extend only to
specific movable or immovable property designated by the statute(s)
creating the privilege. The distinction is much like the distinction between general and special mortgages. *See above* § 10(c)(1). In any
case, once again, a privilege arises only if and to the extent the law
says it does; the law must be express, and privileges are interpreted
strictly against the claimant. Civ. C. art. 3185. This section will outline the (relatively uncommon) general privileges, along with several
special privileges of relatively minor economic importance. The re-
mainder of this chapter will discuss other, more common and economically important special privileges.

(1) General Privileges

The law grants general privileges in all of the debtor's property in favor of those who perform the most socially beneficial acts. Civ. C. arts. 3191, 3252. Here in particular, though, the antiquated nature of this law shines through most brightly. It is often difficult for modern readers to appreciate the social context in which some of these old statutes arose, and the value of the services secured by these privileges is sometimes amusingly limited due to more than a century of inflation. Nonetheless, some of these privileges remain quite relevant today, and an understanding of the range of available privileges provides important context for a complete understanding of this area of the law. These "general" privileges are listed below in their order of priority; that is, privileges discussed first must be paid first before privileges discussed later receive any value from the debtor's property.

(A) Funeral Charges

In the disease-ridden area of New Orleans in the early 1800s, it was of prime importance to get people buried soon after death (for both religious and public health reasons). Therefore, the highest privilege over all of the decedent-debtor's property was given to secure "funeral charges." Civ. C. arts. 3191(1), 3252(1). This privilege is severely limited, though, largely as a result of the law's failure to respond to inflation. This privilege secures *only* the costs of interment (burial) up to a maximum of $500. Civ. C. arts. 3192, 3194. This is a very specific and rather limited privilege, but it reflects the purpose of privilege law generally: Offer an incentive to perform socially necessary acts that might not otherwise be performed immediately without immediate payment.

(B) Law Charges

To avoid rampant destructive litigation, the second highest privilege was granted to secure the winning litigant's right to collect court-ordered "costs" from the losing party at the end of a case. Civ. C. arts. 3191(2), 3252(2). The fact that *this* was considered the second most important goal of privilege law in the 1800s (right behind burying the dead, and ahead of the unpaid costs of a terminal illness) is a chilling commentary on our society, indeed! For this privilege to apply to the losing party's property, the losing side must be taxed with the "costs" of the suit by court order. Civ. C. arts. 3195–96. "Costs" are generally limited to such items as filing fees, copying costs, transcript production costs, and costs incurred in forced execution of the judgment (applying for execution writs, etc.). Costs generally do *not* include the opposing side's attorney's fees. Thus, "law charges" are generally small, so this privilege is quite specific and limited, as well.

(C) Expenses of Last Sickness

To encourage treatment of the rampant disease infecting New Orleans in the early 1800s, the third highest privilege was granted to secure the unpaid health care expenses incurred during the "last sickness" of the debtor or the debtor's dependent children. Civ. C. arts. 3191(3), 3204, 3252(3). The law mentions only the claims of physicians and surgeons, nurses, and "apothecaries" (pharmacists), so it is not clear that general hospital bills would fall within the ambit of this law. Civ. C. art. 3202. "Last," of course, means last—this law contemplates the expenses of the *terminal* illness from which the debtor (or dependent) died. Civ. C. art. 3199. If the sickness lingered over a long time, the privileged expenses include only those that accrued after the debtor was confined to bed or a hospital, and no earlier than one year before death. Civ. C. arts. 3200–01. Note that this privilege is *not* limited in dollar amount, as the funeral expense privilege is. This privilege might conceivably apply today to the unpaid expenses of such resource-intensive and chronic diseases as AIDS and cancer, although if neither private nor social insurance covers these expenses today, the decedent is not likely to have any valuable property to which the privilege might extend.

(D) Servants' Wages and Clerks' Salaries

The final truly "general" privileges extend to all of the "employer's" property to secure the unpaid wages of domestic servants for up to two years, and any unpaid salary of "clerks, secretaries, and other persons of that kind." Civ. C. arts. 3191(4), (6), 3252(4)–(5). With the advent of industrial labor relations and modern laws regulating labor and employment, this privilege has been all but completely supplanted in protecting the rights of unpaid employees. This privilege remains little more than a historical oddity. For example, the "servants" referred to here are those who live in the home of the debtor. Civ. C. art. 3205. Perhaps a live-in nanny would qualify today, although one wonders whether the average nanny would have the economic wherewithal to bring and execute a claim for unpaid wages/salaries.

(E) Open Account Credit for Retail Provisions

One final privilege is "general" only in the sense that it extends to all of the debtor's *movable* property—it does not reach immovables. Civ. C. art. 3191(5). This privilege secures the unpaid purchase price of provisions purchased by the debtor on credit during the past six months from such retailers as "bakers, butchers, and grocers," and during the past year by "keepers of boarding houses and taverns." While one might imagine a local bar seizing the property of someone who had failed to pay his bar tab for the past year, such a situation is undoubtedly uncommon in the extreme. In the 19th century, it was quite common for grocers to sell provisions on "open account" and record each buyer's running balance in a store ledger. This still happens today, particularly in more rural areas of the state, but this type of arrangement has become relatively uncommon. Once again, one doubts that the local grocer would seek to seize the property of a person whose balance remained unpaid for six months, and such people would likely have very little valuable movable property to seize in any event. This privilege is likely of little relevance today.

(F) Spouse/Children in Necessitous Circumstances

One last general privilege provides that, if the debtor dies, leaving a spouse and/or minor children in "necessitous circumstances," that is, owning no property of their own in excess of $1,000, then all such people collectively can demand a payment from the succession of all of the decedent's property to give the claimants a total of $1,000 of property. Civ. C. art. 3252. Note, however, that a mortgage, security interest, or vendor's privilege trumps this privilege, and one suspects that spouses and children in such dire straits would be unable to afford a lawyer to assert this right in any event, let alone to recover only $1,000.

(2) Miscellaneous Special Privileges

All privileges other than those just described are "special." That is, they encumber only the specific property identified in the Code article or statute that creates the privilege. The law creates thousands of privileges covering a wide variety of claims and circumstances, and this book will address only the most common or noteworthy. The following sections will discuss the most prominent such "special" privileges, but a few miscellaneous special privileges that merit brief attention are mentioned in this section. Virtually every state creates privileges (liens) similar to those discussed in this chapter, but a few of these privileges reflect the particular concerns of our local economy (and the particular power of certain interest groups).

(A) Warehouse Keepers and "Depositors"

When one delivers a thing to someone else to hold for a while, this is called a "deposit" in the civil law. For example, most of us "deposit" money with a bank, and we expect the bank to return the money to us later. Similarly, very commonly in the 1800s, and still today, farmers deposit cotton, grain, and other merchandise with a warehouse for storage. The person delivering the item is called a "depositor," and the person holding it is called the "depositary." This arrangement presents at least two sorts of risks from the perspective of each of the parties. First, the depositor might fail to pay for the depositary's costs of storage and preservation of the item. Second, the depositary's creditors might seize and assert rights in the depositor's item, believing it to belong to the depositary. To encourage the socially beneficial practice of storing items for another (and using the storage facilities available), the law provides a series of privileges to protect the interests of both depositors and depositaries.

The law protects the depositary with a privilege in any items stored to secure the depositor's payment of any *expenses* incurred to hold or preserve the thing. Civ. C. arts. 3217(6), 3224–26, 3247. This privilege does *not* secure full payment of the contract price for storage; it covers only the depositary's *expenses* incurred in holding the item. This privilege is only for "money laid out." A different law, however (not a privilege), allows the depositary to refuse to return the item to the depositor absent payment of the contract price of storage. Civ. C. art. 2939. In at least one specific instance, in contrast, the privilege *does* secure the contract price for storage. A warehouse (hangar) that stores an aircraft does enjoy a privilege in the aircraft to secure payment of the contract storage price, although the depositary must file a notice of privilege with the FAA in Oklahoma City and in the mortgage records of the parish where the warehouse (hangar) is located. La. Rev. Stat. 9:4512–13.

Similarly, the law protects the depositor's rights in stored items if they are seized by the depositary's creditors or improperly sold by the depositary. The depositor has a privilege on any stored item to secure its return (assertable against whoever has possession of the item), or on the price of the thing (assertable against the depositary if the depositary improperly sells the item). Civ. C. arts. 3217(5), 3222–23, 3248; *but see* La. Rev. Stat. 10:9-102(a)(20), 9-319 (for large "consignments" potentially treated as security interests, subject to Article 9 of the UCC).

(B) Innkeepers

This privilege is a relic of days gone by. When slow travel by horse and buggy was common, and restaurants were few and far between, travelers ate and slept at inns along their routes of travel. To encourage innkeepers to accommodate weary travelers, the law gave innkeepers a privilege on all of the personal effects that a traveler carried into the inn. This privilege secures payment for lodging, as well as for food and ale and other items provided to the traveler. Civ. C. arts. 3217(8), 3233–34. Although travelers still lodge and dine in "inns" today, credit cards have replaced innkeeper book accounts as the virtually universal source of credit payment. Moreover, because it could only be enforced against property carried into and remaining inside the inn, this privilege was always quite limited in its scope and usefulness.

(C) Carriers

To encourage transportation companies to haul things (particularly when transportation by horse and wagon was a cumbersome and expensive proposition), the law created a privilege for carriers on the things transported to secure payment of the transport charges (including labor, taxes, storage, customs fees, etc.). Civ. C. arts. 3217(9); La. Rev. Stat. 9:4601. The Civil Code privilege exists only while the transported thing remains in the carrier's possession, but the Revised Statute privilege extends the privilege to 180 days after the transportation is accomplished, even if the thing has been delivered to its destination.

(D) Attorney's "Charging Lien"

Alongside the general privilege for "law charges," *see above* § 15(b)(1)(B), the special attorney's privilege suggests that a lawyer's services are socially beneficial only if they result in a recovery of property by the client. The special attorney's privilege in Louisiana extends only to money or other property that the attorney recovers for her client, and it secures any fees and expenses that the lawyer might incur. La. Rev. Stat. 9:5001. Some states' laws offer a privilege on all of the client's papers and other items deposited with an attorney, a so-called "retaining lien." In Louisiana and many other states, the privilege is limited to property recovered in litigation, a so-called "charging lien." Note that the privilege extends only to property recovered by *judgment*, not through a settlement. Another law, however, allows a lawyer to take a contract interest in a client's potential recovery by settlement or otherwise (contingency fee), and this contract interest functions as a special privilege virtually identical to the "judgment" privilege. La. Rev. Stat. 37:218.

(E) Drycleaners, Trauma Care Providers, and Miscellaneous

To these salient special privileges, Louisiana law adds a hodgepodge of more obscure and esoteric miscellaneous special privileges for a variety of creditors. *See, e.g.*, La. Rev. Stat. 9:4621–4755. Many

Selected Privileges   111

of these privileges seem rather amusing—unless, of course, you happen to be the very specific creditor who might benefit from, e.g., one of the following:

- a privilege on sewing machines and pianos purchased on credit
- a 90-day privilege for debts associated with logs and lumber
- a privilege for debts related to harvesting moss
- a 6-month privilege for debts for feeding and caring for horses
- a privilege for repair of jewelry and watches worth less than $10, and
- a 30-day privilege for wages in producing manufactured sugar, syrup, or molasses.

Bear in mind that other laws create other special privileges in scattered places throughout the law. These are just a few of the privileges existing now, and more can be and are created year after year by the legislature.

Two noteworthy final examples benefit drycleaners and health care providers. First, dry cleaners and others who clean or repair rugs, carpets, clothing, and other household goods (such as curtains) have a privilege on these things to secure payment of their cleaning and storage fees and expenses. La. Rev. Stat. 9:4681–89. The privilege is only valid while the item(s) remain(s) in the cleaner's possession, and like a general depositor, the cleaner can refuse to return the item(s) until paid. La. Rev. Stat. 9:4682, 9:4686.

Second, health care providers and ambulance services have a special privilege on any judgment, settlement, or insurance proceeds arising from a treated injury. La. Rev. Stat. 9:4751–55. Notice that the lawyer's claim to such proceeds trumps this privilege. La. Rev. Stat. 9:4752. To establish the privilege, the health care provider or ambulance service has to assert the privilege and demand payment by written notice (by certified mail, return receipt requested) to the injured person, insurance company, or liable party (or better yet, all of them). La. Rev. Stat. 9:4753. Anyone who pays out judgment, settlement, or insurance proceeds to anyone but the privilege creditor after having received this notice is liable for such payment to the privilege creditor. La. Rev. Stat. 9:4754.

§ 16 Privileges (and Security Interests) in Crops—"Agricultural Liens"

We are still a heavily agricultural society, particularly in the middle of the country from Minnesota to Louisiana, so consensual and nonconsensual security devices in crops are both important and common. Several different sources of law govern privileges and security interests in crops, including the Civil Code, the Revised Statutes, mortgage law and Article 9 of the UCC. Understanding the interplay among these various rules and the special *filing* requirement imposed on crop privileges is crucial to proper analysis of this rather complex area of security device law.

(a) Privileges of Laborers, Lenders, and "Overseers"

The law gives a privilege to those involved in producing or financing the current year's crop to secure their wages, salaries, and loans. Lenders and "overseers" enjoy a privilege in the current year's crops and their proceeds to secure any debt arising from credit sales of supplies or money lent and used to finance farm operations, as well as the overseer's annual salary. Civ. C. art. 3217(1). Farm laborers enjoy a super-privilege on the crops (but not, apparently, on their proceeds) that ranks prior to any other crop privilege, and the law also grants laborers a privilege in all other movables "which serve to the working of the farm," such as farm implements and other equipment. Civ. C. art. 3217(3). The term "laborers" here includes only natural individuals—not business entities that provide labor through their employees.

(b) Priority With Respect to Mortgages & Article 9 Security Interests

Recall that a recorded mortgage extends to component parts of the land, which includes crops so long as the mortgagor owns both the land and the otherwise unencumbered crops. Civ. C. art. 463. All crop privileges trump even a prior recorded mortgage, however. Civ. C. art. 3217. If the crops are encumbered by a perfected Article 9 security interest, the crops are "movable by anticipation" and not, therefore, subject to any pre-existing mortgage, Civ. C. art. 474, but a perfected Article 9 security interest in crops also trumps a prior recorded mortgage in any event. *See above* § 8(d); La. Rev. Stat. 10:9-334(i).

Article 9 calls crop privileges "agricultural liens," and it governs agricultural liens as well as security interests. *See* La. Rev. Stat. 10:9-102(a)(5), 9-317, 9-322. Under the non-uniform Louisiana Article 9 provision on this topic, the crop privilege of a laborer is automatically perfected and has first priority over any other privilege or security interest in the crops. La. Rev. Stat. 10:9-309(13), 9-322(g)(1). The crop privilege of a farm lessor (*see below* § 18) has priority *even over a prior perfected security interest* if the lessor has "perfected" its privilege at *any time* by properly filing an "effective financing statement" with respect to its lessor's privilege. La. Rev. Stat. 10:9-322(g)(2); 3:3651-60. If the lessor has not made a proper filing for its crop privilege, its privilege is subordinated to a *perfected* security interest in the crops, but an *unperfected* security interest loses to an unperfected lessor's privilege in crops. La. Rev. Stat. 10:9-322(g)(3)–(4).

(c) Special Filing Rules for Interests in Farm Products (and Standing Timber)

To perfect agricultural liens as well as security interests in farm products (including crops) and standing timber in Louisiana, an "effective financing statement" must be filed in a special "central registry." La. Rev. Stat. 3:3654(E), 3:3656(A). The *form* of an "effective financing statement" is very similar to a UCC-1 financing statement filed as a "fixture filing," *see above* § 3(d). Indeed, a UCC-1 financing statement will suffice as long as it complies with the form and information requirements of the central agricultural lien registry law (including a description of the farm on which the crops are growing, perhaps including the USDA Farm Service Agency (FSA) number). *See* La. Rev. Stat. 3:3654(E), 3:3657(A). Also like for general UCC-1 financing statements, the *place* for filing is in any parish clerk of court's office in the state, regardless of where in Louisiana the crops are located. La. Rev. Stat. 3:3656(A)(1). The clerks transmit such filings to the "central registry" of agricultural liens, much like the UCC records.

§ 17 Artisan's and Repairperson's Privileges

To encourage people to make and repair goods on credit, the law offers such people a privilege to secure payment of the fee for their services. This privilege is set forth in two places in the law—in the Civil Code and in the Revised Statutes—and the scope of the privilege differs dramatically between these two sources. The Civil Code provides a privilege on any thing "repaired or made" by a "workman or artisan" to secure the unpaid price of labor, but only the price of *labor*—not the price for parts, materials, and other expenses—and only so long as the thing remains in possession of the artisan or workman. Civ. C. art. 3217(2).

The Revised Statutes offer an expanded privilege that covers labor *and materials.* Moreover, this *statutory* privilege persists in the thing repaired or made for 120 days from the last day on which materials and/or labor were supplied, or until the artisan/repairperson relinquishes possession of the item, whichever is *later.* La. Rev. Stat. 9:4501–02; *see also* La. Rev. Stat. 9:4511–12 (applying even more flexible rules to artisan's privileges in aircraft). Note well that the 120-day "grace period" is measured from the last day on which work or materials were furnished, *not* from the day on which possession was lost. This 120-day "pursuit" period is increased to *one year* if the repaired item is farm equipment or machinery. La. Rev. Stat. 9:4502(A)(2) (applying the 120-day limit only to purchasers and lenders who buy or take security interests in the farm machinery without knowledge of the repair privilege).

§ 18 Lessor's Privilege

To encourage wealthy landowners to place their immovable property into the stream of commerce (e.g., farmland and buildings for production and residence), the law offers them a privilege to secure the rental price and any other obligation(s) under a lease of immovables. Civ. C. arts. 3217(3), 2707. Since the *immovable* belongs to the lessor, the privilege extends to any *movable* property brought onto the leased immovable property by the lessee. Movable property becomes subject to this privilege only when it is "in or upon" the leased premises, but the privilege persists for 15 days after the lessee removes any movable property from the leased premises, so long as the lessor can still identify the property as belonging to the lessee. Civ. C. art. 2710. Note that Louisiana law contains a specific set of statutes governing the scope and enforcement of the lessor's privilege in items placed in self-storage units. *See* La. Rev. Stat. 9:4756–60.

The lessor's privilege does not extend to movables on the leased premises that belong to *third parties* with no lease interest in the immovable property (e.g., overnight guests or customers having deposited things with a leased repair shop). Nonetheless, if the lessor seizes a third party's property "in or upon the leased property," the lessor does not *know* that the property belongs to a third party, and the third party fails to intervene to assert ownership before the property is sold at judicial auction (pursuant to C. Civ. P. art. 1092), the third party's property is essentially deemed to have belonged to the lessee as a matter of law. Civ. C. art. 2709.

The lessor's privilege *does* extend, however, to the property of *sublessees* who have contracted with the lessee to occupy the premises. The sublessee's property is subject to the lessor's privilege only to the extent that the sublessee is indebted to the principal lessee, and only while the sublessee's movable property remains on the premises (i.e., the lessor has no 15-day "right of pursuit" for the sublessee's property). Civ. C. art. 2708. For example, if Lessee owes $10,000 in overdue rent to Lessor, but Sublessee currently owes only $5000 to Lessee (pursuant to the sublease), only up to $5000 of Sublessee's movable property on the premises is subject to the lessor's privilege. Only Lessee's movable property is subject to the privilege to secure the full $10,000 total overdue rent.

One important distinct issue arises for *farm* leases. Since the farm lessor's privilege extends to the *crops* growing on the leased farmland, Civ. C. art. 2707, the special filing regime applicable to crop interests applies to the farm lessor's privilege in crops (though not to the lessor's privilege in other movables on the farm). *See above* §16(b)–(c). Accordingly, an "effective financing statement" should be filed in the central agricultural lien registry to "perfect" the lessor's privilege in the crops to maintain rank and priority against competing security interests and privileges in the crops. La. Rev. Stat. 10:9-322(g)(2)–(4).

One last point is worthy of special mention. Unlike other privileges and security interests, the lessor's privilege can be destroyed if the lessee goes into bankruptcy. *See* 11 U.S.C. §545(3). Federal bankruptcy law evidently disfavors the statutory security rights of lessors. The protections of the lessor's privilege can be easily obtained today by taking a conventional Article 9 security interest in the lessee's movables, and properly perfected Article 9 security interests survive bankruptcy. *See above* §8(a)(5)(A). Thus, lessors are well advised to seek security interests in their lessee's property rather than relying on the lessor's privilege, particularly if bankruptcy is a potential concern.

§19 Vendor's Privilege

To encourage people to sell things on credit, the law grants a privilege on any movable or immovable property sold on credit, which secures payment of the unpaid purchase price. Civ. C. Arts. 3217(7), 3227, 3249(1). The concept is quite simple, with only two important provisos. First, to preserve the vendor's privilege in an *immovable*, the act of sale—preferably indicating that it was a *credit* sale—must be recorded in the mortgage records (in addition to recordation in the conveyance records to establish the transfer of ownership to the buyer). Civ. C. arts. 3271, 3273.

Second, *movables* are subject to the vendor's privilege only so long as they remain in the possession of the immediate buyer. Civ. C. art. 3217(7), 3227. The Revised Statutes expand this privilege in two ways. First, the privilege in movables sold on credit extends to an *insurance* claim in the event that the unpaid items are destroyed by fire (but not, apparently, in any other manner, such as flood, hurricane, etc.). La. Rev. Stat. 9:4581. To enjoy this extension, however, the vendor must provide written notice to the insurer before the insurance proceeds are disbursed to the policy beneficiary. La. Rev. Stat. 9:4582. Second, for U.S. agricultural products sold on credit, if the buyer immediately transfers the agricultural product to a third party, the unpaid vendor can still enforce the vendor's privilege against the product for 5 *days* after delivery to the original buyer. Civ. C. art. 3227, La. Rev. Stat. 9:4541. However, the vendor's privilege does not extend *at all* to credit sales of fresh or frozen vegetables, seafood, and other perishable food products. La. Rev. Stat. 9:4544. Thus, apparently the primary agricultural products to which the vendor's privilege applies are recently harvested nonperishable products like grain, sugar cane, and cotton. Note once again that the farmer's vendor's privilege in these items is likely subject to the special filing rules for interests in farm products, *see above* § 16(c).

Like with the lessor's privilege, the protections of the vendor's privilege can be obtained today much more effectively by taking a conventional purchase-money security interest or mortgage in the property sold on credit. Conventional PMSIs are not subject to the restrictions and limitations of the vendor's privilege, and as we shall see in the next section, the priority rules strongly favor conventional security interests over most privileges, including the vendor's privilege.

§ 20 Ranking Privileges Against Security Interests and Mortgages

Tables 20.1 and 20.2 summarize the ranking scheme of the primary real security devices we have studied thus far. Note that with respect to privileges, timing is generally unimportant (except in a few circumstances, such as "lien creditors" v. unfiled crop privileges, vendor's privilege on immovables v. mortgages, etc.). The question generally is not *when* a privilege was established, but what *kind* of privilege it is. Privileges rank by *type* rather than by *timing*.

Table 20.1
Ranking of Privileges v. Security Interests & Mortgages
Other Than in Farm Products (Crops)

MOVABLES	IMMOVABLES
Lawyer's "charging lien" privilege in recovered property beats all, including prior perfected UCC9 [9:5001, 37:218]	Vendor's privilege [act of sale must be **recorded** in mortgage records per 3271, 3273] beats prior mortgagee only if recorded within 7/15 days of date of act of sale [3186, 3251, 3274]
Possessory privileges for services/materials provided with respect to movables beat prior perfected UCC9 security interest, unless statute specifically provides otherwise [9-333], e.g., • privilege for **depositary's** expenses [3224, 3226, 3262], • **carrier's** privilege for transport expenses [3217(9), 3265], • **artisan's** privilege for labor costs [3217(2)], • statutes provide otherwise with respect to **prior perfected security interests**, which beat Revised Statute privileges for **repair-people** [9:4501(B), 9:4502(B)], **haulers (carriers)** [9:4601(B)], and **self-storage lessors** [9:4758]	**Prior vendor beats later vendor** [3251] • retroactive priority likely does *not* extend to **prior perfected security interests in component parts** [9-322(h), 9-334]
UCC9 security interest, perfected or not, beats lessor's and vendor's privileges [9:4770(B)] and all non-possessory privileges, unless statute specifically says otherwise [9-322(h)] • **lawyer's privilege** beats all, including UCC9 [9:5001] • other statutes also provide otherwise for specific types of collateral [e.g., 9:4661, **horses**] • **repairperson** and **hauler (carrier)** lose only to vendor's privilege and prior perfected security interests [9:4501(B), 9:4502(B), 9:4601(B)]	• NOTE: Immovables subject to general privileges only if movables insufficient [3253, 3266]

MOVABLES	IMMOVABLES
Necessitous spouse or children privilege in property up to $1000 beats all but vendor's privilege and prior mortgages and security interests [3252, 3254]	**Necessitous spouse or children** privilege in property up to $1000 beats all but vendor's privilege and prior mortgages and security interests [3252, 3254]

Depositor's privilege beats all other privileges [3261]
• but lessor's privilege beats depositor's if lessor does not know about depositor's rights [3260]

Lessor's privilege beats vendor and all general privileges *except* **funeral** charges [3257–58, 3263]

Vendor's privilege beats all general privileges [3263]

General privileges rank in order as listed [3191, 3254]: 1) **Funeral** charges 2) **Law** charges 3) **Last illness** expenses 4) Wages of domestic **servants** 5) **Retail provisions** sold on credit 6) Salaries of **clerks and secretaries**	**General privileges** rank in order as follows [3252, 3270]: 1) **Funeral** charges 2) **Law** charges 3) **Last illness** expenses 4) Wages of domestic **servants** 5) Salaries of **clerks and secretaries** **Mortgages lose** to privileges [3186]

Table 20.2
Ranking of Privileges v. Security Interests & Mortgages
in Farm Products (Crops)

1) **laborers** [10:9-322(g)(1); CC
    3217(3) and final ¶]
2) **overseers** [10:9-322(g)(1); CC
    3217(1) and penult ¶]

auto perfected [10:9-309(13)]

3) **lessors** [10:9-322(g)(2)]
4) **UCC9 security interests, other
    agricultural liens** (inter se, first to
    file/perfect wins) [10:9-322(g)(3)]

if **properly** *perfected* in central ag lien
registry (3:3654(E), 3:3656(A))

5) **lessors** [10:9-322(g)(4)]
6) **UCC9 security interests, other
    agricultural liens** (inter se, first to
    attach wins) [10:9-322(g)(5)]

if *not* **properly perfected** in ag lien
registry

   • *but* "purchase money" privilege
     of lenders and suppliers for **seed
     and labor** beat lessor [3259]
   • *and* "purchase money" privilege
     of lenders, suppliers of farm im-
     plements beat lessor [3259]

Mortgage interest in crops loses to
privileges (filed or not) [3186, 3217]
and to *perfected* UCC9 interests
[9-334(i)]. Indeed, mortgage should
lose to *unperfected* UCC9 and other ag
liens, as well, since encumbered crops
should not be subject to mortgage at
all, as they are "movable by anticipation" [CC 474]

(a) Non-Farm Product Movables

The complex ranking scheme for interests in *non-farm product movables* can be broken down into three main rules (and two sub-rules):

First, Article 9 security interests—*perfected or not*—beat almost every
other security device. This is a major policy decision expressed in La.
Rev. Stat. 9:4770 and 10:9-322(h). Article 9 security interests cede to

competing privileges, however, in two circumstances: If the statute creating the privilege expressly provides that the privilege beats an Article 9 security interest, the specific statute prevails. La. Rev. Stat. 10:9-322(h). For example, the statute creating the lawyer's "charging lien" specifically says that it beats even a prior perfected Article 9 security interest. In addition, if the privilege depends upon *possession* of the affected property as to which the creditor has provided services/materials, such a privilege beats even a prior perfected Article 9 security interest, unless the statute creating the privilege explicitly provides otherwise. La. Rev. Stat. 10:9-333. For example, the possessory Civil Code artisan's privilege securing labor beats *all* security interests, even prior perfected, but the more liberal Revised Statute *repairperson's* privilege (with a 120-day right of "pursuit" and greater security coverage) beats only Article 9 interests *not perfected* before the privilege arose. La. Rev. Stat 9:4501(B), 9:4502(B). The ultimate distinction here is that *actual* possession of the repaired item is required to prevail over a prior perfected Article 9 security interest, and even then only to secure claims for *labor* charges.

Second, the lessor's privileges beats the vendor's privilege. Civ. C. art. 3263.

Finally, the general privileges generally rank last (though the funeral charges privilege beats the lessor's privilege), and they rank among themselves in order as listed in the Code. Civ. C. arts. 3191, 3254, 3257.

(b) Immovables

The ranking scheme for interests in immovables is quite simple, and it also can be broken down into three main rules:

First, a recorded vendor's privilege beats a prior recorded mortgage if the act of credit sale was properly recorded within 7 or 15 days of its date (if the act of credit sale was executed in the same or a different parish, respectively, in which the act must be recorded). Civ. C. arts. 3251, 3274. This is similar to the "PMSI perfected within 20 days" rule, in both policy and function. *See above* §8(c)(3). If the act of credit sale for the vendor's privilege is *not* recorded within that time period, it ranks and has preference over other creditors only from the date of recording.

Second, general privileges are enforceable on immovables only if insufficient value is available to satisfy the privileged claims by attaching the affected *movable* property. Civ. C. arts. 3253, 3266. If general privileges do extend to immovables, they most likely outrank prior mortgages and rank against each other in the order listed in the law. Civ. C. arts. 3186, 3252, 3269–70.

Finally, mortgages rank last against privileges, unless a competing vendor's privilege is recorded beyond the 7- or 15-day grace period discussed above. Civ. C. art. 3186; *see also Lawyers Title Ins. Corp. v. Valteau.* 563 So.2d 260 (La. 1990) (holding that a vendor's privilege beats a prior recorded judicial mortgage against the vendee).

§21 Privileges in Improved Immovables— the Private Works Act

One particular privilege in immovable property deserves closer attention. To encourage people to supply labor and materials for the improvement (construction) of immovable property, the law provides a privilege in the immovable to secure unpaid claims for wages and material supplied on credit. Outside Louisiana, such a privilege is generally called a "mechanic's and materialman's lien" (or "M&M lien"). In Louisiana, such privileges are called by the name of the statute that creates the privilege: Private Works Act privileges. The numbers of claimants and the amounts of secured claims are often quite large in building projects, and payment problems arise in this area relatively frequently, so a closer look at the intricacies of the Private Works Act is well worth the effort.

(a) Overview: The Context and Nature of Private Works Act Privileges

The average construction project involves many people performing many types of jobs. For both commercial and residential construction, each aspect of the building project is likely to require a separate specialist, such as the following:

 • architect to design and draw the plan for the building
 • engineer to survey and test the solidness and level of the ground

- tree removal and landfill experts
- cement workers to pour and smooth the slab (foundation) of the building
- carpenters to build the walls and roof, or steel workers to weld the steel frame
- bricklayers to brick in the building
- drywall crew to hang the interior walls
- flooring experts to put in carpet, wood, and tile flooring
- painters to paint inside and outside
- cabinetmakers
- plumbers
- electricians
- landscapers to put in sod, trees, and shrubs

Each of these experts will likely have its own employees—or even smaller firms—to do the actual work, adding more levels of people to the mix. In addition, lots of people supply building materials to these workers (and some of the experts supply their own materials):

- lumberyard for wood, shingles, nails, and other building materials
- steel mills for heavy beams in large buildings
- equipment lessors for heavy equipment (bulldozers, cranes, portable lights)
- brick and tile yard for sand, gravel, cement, and bricks
- window and door sellers
- plumbing and electrical suppliers for large components
- sign suppliers for large display signs
- light fixture and appliance suppliers
- flooring suppliers
- plant nurseries

The same is true when an existing building is being improved or renovated, although there are likely fewer parties involved in such a project.

   With all of these moving parts, most people and firms interested in building do not attempt to contract directly with all of these separate people. Instead, they hire a "general contractor" ("GC") to complete the job, and the GC manages the swarm of activities and decides whom to hire to do the actual work and supply needed materials. The building owner will likely enter into one contract with the GC, and the GC will, in turn, enter into "sub-contracts" with the people down the chain for each task ("subcontractors" and "sub-subcontractors," etc.).

The problem arises when, as in most cases, the owner pays the price of the work and supplies to the general contractor, who is expected to pay the sub-contractors for their work or supplies, who are then expected to pay their sub-subcontractors and employees for their work or supplies. General contractors are notorious for getting into financial trouble (GC work is a tough business with unpredictable margins) and diverting contract payments from owners for other projects or for completely separate purposes. The subcontractors are then left with an action against the GC, but if the GC is in financial trouble, they have no contract privity with the owner, so they are left holding the bag. This has posed serious problems for hundreds of years. Indeed, the notion of providing protection to workers and suppliers who have subcontracted with a general contractor originated long ago in the Civil Law.

(b) Rights Against the Property Owner and the Property

To address this problem, the law gives a privilege on the immovable that these people have built or improved to secure their charges. Civ. C. arts. 3249(2)–(3). The Civil Code provisions are quite vague, though, and they are for all intents and purposes not really "the law" in this area. Instead, the Louisiana Private Works Act provides the detailed legal framework of rights, protections, and responsibilities. *See* La. Rev. Stat 9:4801–42. The PWA is much like the mechanic's and materialman's lien laws of most other states, although the rules vary slightly from state to state.

The law protects contractors (general and sub) with both a claim against the property owner and a privilege in the property to secure that claim. The law creates a claim against the owner for all amounts owed to laborers, movable lessors, suppliers, and other subcontractors who do not otherwise have contractual privity with the owner. La. Rev. Stat. 9:4802(A). Those with whom the owner has contracted directly ("contractors" per La. Rev. Stat. 9:4807(A)) already have a contract claim, so this provision supplies everyone involved in a building project with a personal and unlimited claim against the owner. The "contractor" (e.g., the GC) must indemnify the owner against subcontractors' claims, La. Rev. Stat. 9:4802(F), but this is of little use when the GC is insolvent—which is often precisely the scenario that creates the need for subcontractors' claims and privileges under the PWA.

To secure all of these claims, the law provides a privilege on the immovable constructed, repaired, or improved to everyone involved in supplying labor, materials, or equipment to the project. La. Rev. Stat. 9:4801, 9:4802(B). Note that these claims and privileges affect only the "owner" who contracted with the GC for the construction or improvement—co-owners are not liable, and their interests in the property are not affected by the privilege. 9:4806(B). Similarly, if the "owner" is a lessee or servitude holder, the privilege attaches only to the lease or servitude interest. 9:4806(C)–(D).

(c) Owner's Defense: Notice of Contract and Bond

Technically, the law requires for every construction project that a notice of contract be filed in the mortgage records of the parish where work is to be done (most likely by the GC). La. Rev. Stat. 9:4811(A), 9:4831. The notice must be signed by the owner and the GC, identifying them by name and mailing address, it must contain a legal description of the property (street addresses are insufficient) and a name for the building project, and it must describe the work to be done, the contract price (or an estimate and a description of how the price will be finally calculated), and the expected date of payment (including final payment date for retainage).

Owners have an incentive to make sure this notice of contract is filed. Owners can avoid both personal liability to PWA claimants and the potential attachment of PWA privileges to their property by ensuring that a "notice of contract" and a sufficient bond are filed before work begins on a construction project. *See below* § 21(e); La. Rev. Stat. 9:4802(C). The notice must be reinscribed every five years if the job lasts longer than that. La. Rev. Stat. 9:4834. The requirements for the amount and nature of the protective bond are set forth in La. Rev. Stat. 9:4812. This bond is a promise, generally by a bonding company ("surety"), that the surety will pay a certain specified amount to all potential PWA claimants (if the GC fails to do so). The law absolves the owner of liability in exchange for this promise by the surety to bear a legally defined portion of the potential liability for unpaid PWA claims.

Bonding companies do not accept this potential liability lightly. They generally require significant payment for the issuance of the bond, along with security (collateral from the GC or owner) that the surety will be repaid if demand is made on the bond. This adds significant expense to a construction job, so generally only commercial projects are "bonded." Most smaller residential jobs today are not bonded (although some wealthy people building dream houses might use this process). The bond is too expensive or unavailable at all for smaller GCs with no collateral or poor credit doing small residential building. Indeed, most residential construction in Louisiana is not pursued by an owner contracting with the GC ahead of time at all. Instead, contractors build "spec houses" according to a common plan, and the GC or an affiliated developer owns the lot and house until a realtor sells it. Under these circumstances, the later owner will never face claims from subcontractors, but if the owner buys the property from a GC or developer who has not paid all subcontractors, privileges may remain on the property. Rooting out and satisfying these privileged claims is part of pre-sale due diligence by buyers.

(d) Filing Requirements, Enforcement, and Ranking of PWA Privileges

To preserve their privileges, all PWA claimants must file timely notice of their claims with the recorder of mortgages for the parish where the immovable is located. Civ. C. art. 3272. They must also take additional action timely to enforce their privileges against the property. Four issues arise for PWA claimants seeking to preserve and enforce their claims: 1) *what* must be filed, 2) *when* should it be filed, 3) how can a claimant *enforce* the privilege against the property, and

4) how do these privileges *rank* if not enough value is available in the property to cover all privileged claims. This section will address each of these four issues.

(1) What to File

To preserve both the *claim* and the *privilege* granted by the PWA, claimants must file a "statement of claim" in the mortgage records of the parish where the immovable is located. La. Rev. Stat. 9:4822. If the claimant has no contract privity with the owner, and notice of contract was timely filed, a copy of the statement of claim must also be delivered to the owner at the address listed in the notice of contract. La. Rev. Stat. 9:4822(A). The statement of claim must be in writing and signed by the claimant or the claimant's agent, it must identify the immovable by legal description, *see* La. Rev. Stat. 9:4831(C), and it must describe the dollar amount claimed and the nature of the work, reasonably itemizing elements like the person contracted with and specific materials or services supplied. *See* La. Rev. Stat. 9:4822(G).

Certain claimants must provide or file additional documents, as well, to preserve their privileges. First, if the total price of the project is over $25,000, a notice of contract must have been timely filed (but not necessarily a bond) in order for the general contractor to enjoy *any* privilege in the immovable. La. Rev. Stat. 9:4811(D). Second, lessors of movables (e.g., bulldozers, portable lights, etc.) who do *not* have contractual privity with the owner must deliver a copy of the lease to the owner and the general contractor no later than 10 days after the leased movables are first placed on the premises. La. Rev. Stat. 9:4802(G). Third, all suppliers of movables for residential construction (e.g., the lumberyard, brickyard, etc.) must deliver by registered or certified mail, return receipt requested, notice of non-payment to the owner at least 10 days before filing a statement of claim (and no later than 75 days after the last day of the month when their movables were delivered to the worksite, contractor, or sub-contractor, or expiration of lien filing period, if notice of contract was recorded). La. Rev. Stat. 9:4802(G)(2)–(3). Finally, surveyors, engineers, and architects without contractual privity with the owner must give notice to the owner within 30 days of execution of their (written) employment agreement. La. Rev. Stat. 9:4801(5), 9:4802 (A)(5)(b).

(2) When to File

The time limit for filing a statement of claim depends upon four things: (1) whether or not notice of contract was timely filed for the project, (2) whether or not the claimant has contractual privity with the owner, (3) whether or not notice of termination is filed after completion of the project, and (4) when the project reaches "substantial completion." The filing and form requirements for a "notice of termination" are set forth in the statute. *See* La. Rev. Stat. 9:4822(E)–(F). This notice allows the owner to start the clock running for the filing of PWA claims and privileges, though not before default by the general contractor or "substantial completion" of at least a distinct portion of the project.

"Substantial completion" is thus the key concept here. The law defines "substantial completion" in practical terms that reflect the often vague concluding stage of a building project. A project is substantially complete when the "last work" is performed or materials delivered to the project *or* (probably more commonly) when the owner "accepts" the improvement or "occupies" the construction, even if some minor work remains to be done. La. Rev. Stat. 9:4822(H). Contractors are seldom in a position to deliver perfection, and they have powerful incentives to move on to the next construction job as quickly as possible. Consequently, when the contractor deems a construction project to have concluded, the owner often identifies a number of relatively minor things remaining to be done (paint touch-up, grouting touch-up, small repairs to electric and plumbing, etc.). Generally, after the contactor says the job is done, the owner does a "walk-through" and makes a "punch list" of small deficiencies to be cleaned up before the owner will accept the job (and perhaps before the owner will pay out the "retainage" final payment being held pending completion). The owner, then, remains largely in control of when "substantial completion" occurs (and when the clock starts running on the filing of PWA statements of claim). If the owner accepts the project, it is substantially complete, but if the owner insists on the completion of a punch-list of items before accepting the job, the project will be complete only after the last work is performed to satisfy these demands. Once again, only after the project is "substantially complete" (or the contractor defaults) may the owner file a notice of termination.

PWA claimants have 60 days after "substantial completion" or the filing of a notice of termination to file their statements of claim in three cases. Those with contractual privity with the owner *always* have 60 days to file their statements. La. Rev. Stat. 9:4822(B), (D). Claimants without contractual privity with the owner have 60 days to file their statements if a notice of contract was not timely filed *or* if a notice of termination was not filed after a notice of contract had been timely filed. La. Rev. Stat. 9:4822(C). Also, if notice of contract was not timely filed, suppliers of movables for residential construction get 70 days. La. Rev. Stat. 9:4822(D)(2). Note well that the time for filing in all cases is measured from completion of the entire project (or at least a distinct portion of it, identified in the contract or in a notice of termination), *not* from completion of any individual claimant's task within the project.

If a notice of contract was timely filed *and* a notice of termination was also filed, claimants without contractual privity with the owner must file their statements of claim no later than 30 days after the filing of the notice of termination. La. Rev. Stat. 9:4822(A), (J). This is yet another incentive for the owner to ensure that at least a notice of contract (if not also a bond) along with a notice of termination is timely filed for any building project.

(3) Enforcement of PWA Privileges

Like other privileges, the PWA privilege offers only a reservation of rights in property to secure claims that are judicially established through ordinary process—it does not offer any advantages in efficiency in the enforcement process (such as executory process, which is available only for Article 9 security interests and certain mortgages). Not only that, though, the enforcement process for PWA privileges requires *more* formalities within relatively tight deadlines.

In addition to filing a statement of claim within the 30- or 60-day period discussed above, PWA claimants must commence an action against the owner to enforce their claims or privileges within one year of the expiration of the time for filing the corresponding statement of claim. La. Rev. Stat. 9:4823(A)(2). If the owner has timely filed a notice of contract and posted a bond, a PWA claimant must initiate an action against the surety within this same time limit to assert rights against the bond proceeds. La. Rev. Stat. 9:4813(E).

After initiating an action to enforce the privilege, PWA claimants must *also* file a notice of "*lis pendens*" (Latin for "suit pending," *see* C. Civ. P. art. 3752) in the mortgage records of the parish where the immovable is located. This notice of lis pendens must be filed within one year after the *filing of the statement of claim*—not one year after expiration of the period for filing the statement of claim. La. Rev. Stat. 9:4833(E). This could act as a trap for the unwary. A notice of lis pendens cannot be filed until an action is commenced. Thus, claimants who file their statements of claim before the expiration of the time to do so must initiate an action earlier, to be able to file the notice of lis pendens within one year to protect their rights in the property against competing third parties.

(4) Ranking and Priority of PWA Privileges

The ranking scheme of PWA privileges and other security devices in immovables can be divided into three relatively distinct parts: (1) certain privileges rank first, regardless of timing; (2) other PWA privileges rank against mortgages by timing; and (3) PWA privileges rank against each other by type. This section will address these three sets of rules in order.

(A) Laborer's Privilege Always Ranks "First"

The properly recorded and enforced privileges of *laborers* (individual employees of the owner, a contractor, or a subcontractor) beat all private claimants under the PWA, including prior recorded mortgages and vendor's privileges, regardless of timing. La. Rev. Stat. R.S. 9:4821(2). The PWA exists primarily to protect the rights of individuals who have supplied their most valuable commodity—their energy and industry—to a building project. Therefore, the law provides such claimants the highest level of protection in every case (assuming, of course, that these claimants have preserved their rights with the required filings, which may well not always be the case).

Note that "first" here does not necessarily mean "first." Not surprisingly, the privileges of state and local authorities for certain taxes and improvement claims (weed abatement, etc.) trump every other privilege, including the laborer's privilege. La. Rev. Stat. 9:4821(1). But even if these privileges are present, they are generally not so great as to absorb most of the value of the immovable.

(B) Non-Laborer's PWA Privileges v. Mortgages/Vendors

For non-laborer PWA privilege claimants who have successfully maneuvered the hurdles of timely filing statements of claim, initiating lawsuits, and filing notices of lis pendens, the rules of priority between PWA privileges and competing mortgages (and vendor's privileges, although see Civ. C. art. 3268) often lead to disappointment. The rules strongly favor and protect mortgagees, at least those sophisticated enough to have followed the rules. Non-laborer PWA privileges rank against mortgages according to the timing of when the mortgage was recorded and when the project (called the "work," La. Rev. Stat. 9:4808(A)) began. Whichever occurred first in time, this determines whether the mortgagee stands ahead of or behind the non-laborer PWA privilege holders. *See* La. Rev. Stat. 9:4820(A), 9:4821(3)–(6).

If notice of contract was timely filed, the project is deemed to have begun upon filing, and that point in time establishes the ranking date against mortgages for *all PWA privilege claimants* (except laborers). La. Rev. Stat. 9:4820(A)(1). Just as the time for filing a statement of claim is not measured from *conclusion* of any individual claimant's work, the ranking of privileges is not measured from the *beginning* of any individual claimant's work. Rather, both are measured from the beginning and end of the *entire project* (or distinct, identified portions of the project). For projects that can be broken into stages, if the owner or GC files separate notices of contract *and* separate bonds for each stage, each stage can be considered a separate "work" with a separate beginning and ending timeline for filing and ranking privileges. La. Rev. Stat. 4808(B).

If notice of contract was *not* timely filed, the central question is when the project began. La. Rev. Stat. 9:4820(A)(2). For most jobs and most claimants, the "work" begins when materials worth more than $100 are delivered to the worksite (e.g., a bundle of wood for cement forms is dropped onto the lot) or "other work" is conducted on the site that is "visible from a simple inspection and reasonably indicates that work has begun." La. Rev. Stat. 9:4820(A)(2). So-called "dirt work" is not considered "other work" that establishes the priority date, however. If, as often happens in the pre-construction stage of a project, a contractor clears trees or levels ground by adding fill dirt or carving away hills, this "dirt work" is not "work" that sets the priority date of PWA privileges. The same is true if an architect does measuring and planning work, a surveyor surveys the lot, or an engineer drives test pilings to test the firmness of the ground. Indeed, if architects, surveyors, and engineers perform such preparatory work, that activity might constitute a separate "work," but the privileges of such architects, surveyors, or engineers rank only from the time they file their statements of claim, not from commencement of their separate preparatory "work." La. Rev. Stat. 4808(C), 9:4822(D)(1)(b).

For the mortgagee hoping to record a mortgage and establish priority over any eventual PWA privileges, then, determining whether or not "work" has begun on a site is crucial. The law aids mortgagees here again by offering them a sure way to establish that "work" has not begun when they record their mortgages. The mortgagee can obtain a "no-work affidavit" from an engineer, surveyor, architect, or building inspector stating that the person visited the construction site on a specific date and neither work nor materials were present that would indicate the commencement of "work." La. Rev. Stat. 9:4820(C). If this affidavit is filed in the mortgage records within 4 business days of its execution by the affiant, and the mortgage is recorded before or within 4 business days after the affidavit is filed, the mortgage will as a matter of law beat any PWA privileges arising before execution of the affidavit (technically, the law says that no PWA claimant can controvert the correctness of the affidavit as to when "work" began). Thus, if "work" really had begun earlier, the mortgagee nonetheless enjoys priority, but the *affiant* is liable to the PWA claimants for any loss they suffer as a result of their privileges' being subordinated to the mortgagee's rights as a result of the false affidavit.

(C) Priority Among Non-Laborer PWA Privileges

Whether they beat the mortgagee or not, the non-laborer PWA claimants rank against each other according to which of two categories they occupy (and pro-rata for two or more claimants that fall into the same category). La. Rev. Stat. 9:4821(4)–(5). The first, higher priority group includes subcontractors (those without contractual privity with the owner), all suppliers of movables, and all lessors of movables. The second, lower priority group includes all other claimants who contracted directly with the owner; i.e., the general contractor and owner-hired architects, surveyors, and engineers (along with their "professional subconsultants," who are not technically in contract privity with the owner).

(e) Owner Options for Dealing With PWA Privileges

When financial trouble strikes a building project and privileges are recorded against the property, the owner must somehow deal with these privileges or risk losing the property (or at the very least, risk being left with unmarketable title). The owner must have the privileges removed from the records. For *improperly* filed or *ineffective* privileges, the law allows the owner to demand written authorization from the claimant for removal of the privilege, or to initiate a summary proceeding to have the privilege declared improper. La. Rev. Stat. 9:4833. But claimants with properly filed and effective privileges must be satisfied.

Owners have essentially three options for removing valid privilege records from the chain of title for the property. First, the owner can simply pay off the claimants. As frustrating as it might be to pay subcontractors after already having paid the defalcating GC, this is often the only reasonably option for "redeeming" the property from PWA claimants. Alternatively, to have the privilege records cancelled more quickly, the owner can deposit with the recorder of mortgages a bond, cash, or CDs worth 125% of the total of all filed PWA claims (pending negotiation and final payment of the claimants). La. Rev. Stat. 9:4823(D), 9:4835. This is not a particularly appealing option, either, but it has the benefit of immediacy.

The law offers "responsible" owners a much more attractive option, and this is the most powerful incentive for owners to file a notice of contract and bond before initiation of a building project, as discussed above. If notice of contract and a sufficient bond were timely filed, *see above* §21(c), the owner can initiate a suit for a determination of the validity of the PWA claims and privileges (after the period for filing statements of claim has expired). La. Rev. Stat. 9:4841(A)–(D). This suit is called a "concursus" action (outside Louisiana, the term generally used is "interpleader"). Essentially, all PWA claimants are haled into court and asked to establish the validity of their claims and to challenge (if they can) the legal sufficiency of the filed notice of contract and bond. The owner can have all claimants ordered to show cause why the notice of contract and bond should not release the owner from liability altogether (i.e., what legal deficiencies exist in the notice or bond). If the notice and bond were timely filed, the court should enter an order discharging the owner of liability and ordering the recorder to cancel the privileges recorded against the property (leaving the claimants to assert their rights against the bond). La. Rev. Stat. 9:4841(D). As mentioned above, filing a bond increases the expense of a building project significantly, but the incentive for owners to shield themselves and their property from potential PWA claims and privileges can be equally significant.

Chapter 4

Suretyship

§22 Introduction, Creation of the Suretyship Contract

(a) Introduction

Until now, we have studied consensual and nonconsensual accessory *real* rights (in property) that secure principal obligations. Now we turn to a final, somewhat different security device, a *personal* right that is always consensual. "Suretyship" is an accessory contract (like an Article 9 security interest or conventional mortgage) by which a person (called the "surety" or "guarantor") binds him or herself (not specific property) to a creditor to fulfill the obligation(s) of another person (the "principal obligor") upon the failure of the latter to do so. Civ. C. art. 3035. Now, instead of reserving a right in certain property ahead of time, the creditor seeks to add contingent obligors as security, to be able to enforce the personal promises of other people who are perhaps more creditworthy than the principal obligor. This personal right against the surety (guarantor) is enforced like any other contract. Note that the surety's suretyship obligation can itself be secured by a real security right in the surety's property, as well. Security devices often occur in combination like this in the real world, which is one of the reasons why this book treats them all together.

One of the most common circumstance where one might encounter suretyship in practice is when a small business wants to borrow money from a bank. Recall that the law of business associations (e.g., corporations, LLCs, LLPs, etc.) provides limited liability to the entity's constituents, shielding the owners from business debts. Therefore, a bank considering whether to lend to a limited liability entity will look first only to the business entity's assets and debt history in determining the borrower's creditworthiness. Small businesses, in particular, will often not be able to get a loan based solely on their own poor or sparse credit, and small businesses may own little valuable property in which they might offer *real* security rights. Suretyship allows the bank to avoid the limited liability law by tying the business's owners (or others) *personally* to the loan (but only *secondarily*) by getting them to guarantee payment of the loan if the business entity defaults. This also aligns the interests of the business's owners with the fate of the business and the loan. Rather than walking away from the loan obligation and hiding behind the "veil" of limited liability when the business entity faces financial trouble, leaving the bank's loan unpaid, owner-*sureties* have a personal incentive to reinvigorate the business and ensure that the guaranteed loan obligation is fulfilled.

Another common scenario involving suretyship is the very common practice of a parent guaranteeing a car loan for a child. Even if the value of the car is sufficient to make a purchase-money security interest in the car adequate security, the lender may not want to deal with the complications of repossession and foreclosure. *See above* §9. Getting a parent with better creditworthiness (and more available future income and other assets) to guarantee the loan is a very effective and efficient means of securing repayment of the car loan.

Like other security devices, suretyship can be used to secure *any* principal obligation—past, present, or future, definite or indefinite—although most secure repayment of money debts ("all indebtedness of any kind of principal obligor to bank arising at any time, past, present, or future"). Civ. C. art. 3036. The guaranteed obligation is the "principal obligation," while the suretyship contract is an accessory obligation.

(b) Creation of the Suretyship Contract

The two formal requirements for creating a suretyship contract are quite simple: The contract must be express and in writing. Civ. C. art. 3038.

(1) In Writing

The writing requirement should be the same as for mortgages, with the same potential exceptions for electronic records today. *See above* § 10(b)(1). An additional requirement that the contract be "signed" is understood here, as the writing must evidence that a specific obligor has undertaken the suretyship obligation. An act under private signature is sufficient, Civ. C. art. 1837, although an authentic act has some minor advantages even here (such as the "self-proving" nature of the signature).

(2) Express

The requirement that the contract be "express" simply means that any ambiguity as to the duties undertaken in the contract will be interpreted *not* to create a suretyship. It must be clear that the surety has actually promised to pay the principal obligation if the principal obligor does not. Anything less clear than "I will pay if the obligor does not" is not good enough. A written statement like "I assure you that the obligor will pay," for example, does not clearly indicate that the writer will pay if the obligor does not. Suretyship cannot be implied from context; the existence and terms of the suretyship K must be clear from the four corners of the writing. The law emphasizes that parole evidence is not admissible to "establish … a promise to pay the debt of a third person." Civ. C. art. 1847.

On the other hand, suretyship arises by *contract*, so virtually any element of the contract other than "I will pay if the obligor does not" may be "qualified, conditioned, or limited in any lawful manner." Civ. C. art. 3040. The form requirements above may not be waived, but the legal *effects* of suretyship can be altered or suspended by contract (e.g., the surety's ability to assert the defenses discussed below). *See below* § 24(d).

(3) "Implied" Suretyship of Ostensible Principals

Although a writing that is ambiguous about the promise of one party to pay the debts of another will *not* be interpreted to create a suretyship obligation, some writings in which one party clearly promises to pay a debt on which someone else is liable *are* governed by suretyship rules even if the parties framed the transaction otherwise. Specifically, someone who has signed a contract as a co-obligor may be treated as a *surety* (with a surety's rights and defenses) rather than a solidarily liable co-obligor. For example, parents who are called on to "co-sign" vehicle notes with their children are often asked to sign as solidarily liable co-obligors, although the nature of the transaction is really a suretyship: The parent is simply promising to repay money lent to someone else, without receiving any of the direct value of the loan she is undertaking to repay as a co-obligor.

The parent or other co-obligor in such a situation does not appear to be able to assert any of the rights and defenses of a surety, as she is a principal obligor according to the contract. But the parent or other co-obligor will nonetheless be *treated* as a surety, entitled to all of the rights and defenses of a surety, if two factors are present. Civ. C. art. 3037. First, the "principal cause" of the contract must be to guarantee performance of the obligation. As just mentioned, the principal—and perhaps the only—cause of a parent's undertaking to act as "co-obligor" on a child's car note in most cases is to guarantee to the lender that the loan will be repaid (to entice the lender to make a loan to the child, which the child will repay entirely on his or her own under normal circumstances). Second, for the "co-obligor" to be treated as a surety, the creditor must "clearly know" that the two ostensible principal obligors are *really* a principal obligor and someone "standing behind" the principal obligor's debt. Substance overcomes form here—if the lender *knows* that the parent is essentially guaranteeing the child's note (which will often be the case), the parent will be treated as a surety no matter how the contract is signed, and the creditor will be subject to the parent's suretyship defenses, if any. *See below* §24.

§23 Surety's Rights Against the Principal Obligor and Other Sureties

If the surety is called on to perform the guaranteed obligation, the law arms the surety with a series of rights to hold the principal obligor responsible. As a matter of law, whether or not the principal obligor agrees to—or even *knows about*—the surety's involvement, the law allows the surety to enforce the now satisfied principal obligation against the principal obligor. After all, the principal obligor is *primarily* liable and has presumably obtained some benefit from the creditor, for which the surety will have paid. Even if the surety is remunerated for acting as surety (and not all sureties are paid for this "service"), the principal obligor might be unjustly enriched if she is not bound to make the surety whole (if she is able).

If more than one surety is involved, the rules allocating responsibility among solidary obligors apply. So if one surety is called on to pay the entire guaranteed obligation to the creditor, that surety has rights not only against the debtor, but also against the other co-sureties. Optimally, the debtor might pay to make the surety whole again, but if the debtor cannot pay or be forced to pay, a surety's rights against co-sureties is a second-best protection. This section discusses both of these sets of rights enjoyed by sureties.

(a) Rights Against the Principal Obligor

As one would expect based on prevailing notions of fairness, if the surety is required to pay the principal obligation, the law requires the principal obligor to repay the surety if at all possible (whether or not the surety has been paid separately for providing the "service" of acting as surety). Two provisions accomplish this goal, one simply and directly, and one indirectly but with the potential for some extra "lagniappe" rights. These two provisions allow the surety to seek "reimbursement" and "subrogation" to the creditor's rights. Civ. C. art. 3047.

(1) Reimbursement

The most basic rule simply entitles the surety to demand that the principal obligor reimburse the surety for what she was required to pay the creditor on the principal obligor's behalf. Civ. C. art. 3049. The only wrinkle here is that, if the surety paid the obligation to the creditor in advance of its due date (probably through some error), the surety can demand reimbursement only after the obligation is "due and exigible" (i.e., currently subject to payment). Of course, if the principal obligor is insolvent by this time, the surety will suffer a loss.

Trouble might arise here in two other cases, as well. The first is when the surety pays an obligation that is not enforceable against the principal obligor. If the obligation was not enforceable due to some defense of the principal obligor (presumably excluding defenses based on lack of capacity or discharge in bankruptcy, *see* Civ. C. art. 3046), but the surety paid the obligation despite this defense, the surety can seek reimbursement from the principal obligor only if the principal obligor "was apprised" that the creditor was still demanding payment, or if the surety at least "made a reasonable effort to notify the principal obligor" of the creditor's demands. Civ. C. art. 3050. Optimally, if the principal obligor learns of the creditor's collection efforts, she will inform the surety, who will assert the defense and refuse payment. Civ. C. art. 3046.

Second, not only should the surety check with the principal obligor *before* paying, the surety should notify the principal obligor *after* paying, as well. If the surety pays on any obligation, and the principal obligor later pays *again* because she did not receive notice of the surety's earlier payment, the surety will lose the right to seek reimbursement from the principal obligor on *any basis*. Civ. C. art. 3051. Of course, the surety can still seek return of her payment from the *creditor* (perhaps based on enrichment without cause), but this is an inconvenience the surety can and should easily avoid.

The surety's right to seek reimbursement from the principal obligor might not be very valuable if the principal obligor divests herself of all property or absconds shortly after the surety pays on her behalf. To offer the surety some protection in advance, the law allows the surety to demand security from the principal obligor to secure her reimbursement obligation (e.g., a security interest or mortgage in the principal obligor's property). Civ. C. art. 3053. Certain conditions must exist before the surety can demand security, but these conditions are quite expansive. If the principal obligor refuses to offer security, the law further empowers the surety to sue to compel the production of security. Civ. C. art. 3054. This suit, of course, wastes both time and money, in a sense exacerbating the same problem it is trying to avoid (i.e., the surety's laying out money that she might be unable to collect from the principal obligor). This right to demand security may well be of little value in most cases, but it bears keeping in mind.

(2) Subrogation

In addition to asserting her *own* right to reimbursement of payments to the creditor, the surety can also assert whatever rights the *creditor* had against the principal obligor under the obligation at issue. This right of the surety to "stand in the shoes" of the creditor is called "subrogation." Civ. C. arts. 1825, 1829(3), 3048. Subrogation gives the surety the right to exercise *all* of the rights that the creditor had against the principal obligor on the obligation.

This may produce some "lagniappe" rights for the surety. For example, if the principal obligor had granted the creditor real security rights in her property to secure the debt (e.g., a security interest or mortgage), the surety standing in the shoes of the creditor by subrogation can enforce those security rights if the debtor fails to pay the obligation. Civ. C. art. 1826(A). If the surety paid only part of the obligation, however, the surety's right to collect through subrogation is subordinated (takes a back seat) to the creditor's remaining right to payment. Civ. C. art. 1826(B). Moreover, the surety can collect from the principal obligor only so much as she paid to the creditor, although a surety suing on the debt through subrogation can collect attorney's fees and later accrued interest on the debt, as long as the principal obligation contract provided for such recovery. Attorney's fees and interest are *not* generally available, in contrast, to a surety asserting only her own reimbursement right. *See* Civ. C. art. 3052 cmt. (c).

(b) Rights Against Co-Sureties

If multiple sureties have guaranteed an obligation, a surety who is required to pay can seek not only full reimbursement from the principal obligor, but also partial reimbursement from the other co-sureties (unless the sureties have agreed otherwise). Whether asserted directly or through subrogation to the creditor's rights, the surety's action against a co-surety is called an action for "contribution." Civ. C. art. 3056. While a surety generally can seek full reimbursement from the principal obligor, co-sureties are liable to each other only for a specific share of the whole obligation, and a paying surety can collect only the unpaid shares of other sureties. The shares of each of the co-sureties are deemed to be equal per capita ("virile shares") unless the sureties have agreed otherwise (orally or in writing). Civ. C. art. 3055.

Complications arise if one or more sureties become insolvent and thus unable to contribute to a paying surety. If one surety becomes insolvent, so that her share cannot be collected, the shares are reallocated among the remaining sureties per capita, as if the insolvent surety had never existed. Civ. C. art. 3056. For example, if four sureties guarantee one obligation, and one surety is called upon to pay 100% to the creditor, she generally can seek contribution of 25% from each of the other three sureties. If one of the three non-paying sureties has become insolvent, the virile shares are reallocated among three instead of four solvent sureties, so the paying surety can collect 33% from the two remaining solvent sureties. The contribution liability of the solvent sureties has risen from 25% to 33%, but so has the amount that the paying surety will have to bear herself, as a result of the exclusion of the insolvent surety.

In addition, if the paying surety is clever enough to pay less than 100% of the principal obligation yet negotiate a release of co-sureties, the co-sureties are liable to the paying surety for their virile shares of the amount *actually paid*. For example, if four sureties have guaranteed one debt of $100,000, and one surety negotiates a full release of all of the sureties in exchange for payment of $80,000, that surety can collect contribution from each of the remaining sureties of $20,000 (leaving her with an unreimbursed payment of $20,000, also). Normally, each surety would be liable for 25% of the entire obligation—$25,000—but if one surety obtains a benefit for the others, the benefit is shared among all (reducing the amount each has to pay).

§24 Surety's Defenses Against the Creditor

By expressly agreeing to pay, the surety agrees that the only suspensive condition to her suretyship obligation is the principal obligor's default, which usually but not always means simply failure to pay the debt when due. *Se above* §9(a). A surety may well be able to assert certain defenses to payment against the creditor, however, although these defenses are often waived in commercial suretyship agreements. This section discusses the defenses that a surety *does* and does *not* have against the creditor's demand for payment.

(a) No Division or Discussion

The law explicitly deprives sureties of two specific defenses that they might assert against the creditor: "division" and "discussion." Civ. C. art. 3045. Unless the suretyship contract specifically says otherwise, each surety is liable to the creditor for the performance of 100% of the guaranteed obligation as soon as the debtor defaults.

"Division" would allow the surety to "divide" her liability to the creditor by the number of other sureties. For example, if four co-sureties agreed to guarantee an obligation, a defense of "division" would allow each surety to refuse to pay the creditor more than her "virile share" of 25%. The law now explicitly provides that co-sureties are solidary co-obligors as a matter of law, which can be modified only by an express provision in the suretyship agreement.

"Discussion" would allow a surety to demand that the creditor un-successfully attempt to enforce the obligation against the principal obligor before seeking performance from the surety. Only if the principal obligor were clearly insolvent or no valuable property could be found on which to execute a judgment would the surety be liable. Some suretyship contracts provide for such a limitation, in which case the arrangement is called a "guarantee of collection." Such restrictive terms are relatively rare in guarantee agreements today. As a matter of law, all suretyship contracts today presumptively create "guarantees of payment." That is, as soon as the principal obligor is in default, the suretyship obligation is enforceable immediately. The creditor can sue either the principal obligor or the surety or both, at the lender's discretion.

(b) Defenses of the Principal Obligor, Including Remission

Sureties *can* assert a number of other defenses against the creditor. First, the surety can assert any defenses that the principal obligor could assert, *except for* lack of capacity and discharge in bankruptcy of the principal obligor. Civ. C. art. 3046. So for example, if the principal obligation was the product of duress or fraud against the principal obligor, for example, the surety can assert these defenses against payment to the creditor. On the other hand, one of the primary purposes of obtaining an accessory security right from a creditworthy source (the surety) is to avoid the adverse effects of the principal obligor's potential bankruptcy or to overcome a capacity restriction, so excluding these defense makes perfect sense.

Similarly, just like accessory *real* security rights like mortgages and privileges, suretyship is an *accessory* obligation, so the suretyship obligation is extinguished if the *principal* obligation is extinguished. Civ. C. arts. 3058–59. Thus, if the principal obligation prescribes, or if the creditor contractually remits (releases) the principal obligor's liability, all accessory suretyship obligations are extinguished. Civ. C. art. 1892.

If the creditor remits not the principal obligor, but rather one of a number of co-sureties, the issue is a bit more complicated. After a revision in the late 1980s, the law is now clear that releasing a surety simply remits the other sureties, and *only* to the extent that the other sureties might have recovered *contribution* from the released surety. Civ. C. art. 1892. Recall that this contribution portion is presumptively each surety's "virile" per capita share of the unpaid principal obligation. *See above* §23(b). By default, then, if any surety is released, that surety's virile share is released, but only as to the other sureties. For example, if four sureties have guaranteed an obligation, and the creditor remits one of them in exchange for payment of 10% of the principal obligation, the creditor is deemed to have actually released that surety's entire virile share, so the other three sureties remain liable for only 75% of the principal obligation (divided equally among them, unless otherwise agreed). Of course, the creditor can still collect the unpaid 90% of the principal obligation from the principal obligor, if possible.

Once again, insolvency of a surety further complicates the situation. In our example above, if a second of the four sureties had become insolvent *after* the creditor had released the first surety for payment of 10% of the guaranteed debt, for how much would the other two sureties remain liable? The analysis might proceed chronologically as follows: Release of the first surety released her 25% virile share, regardless of the amount collected from her (leaving one-third of the remaining 75% of the original principal obligation—25%—to each of

the three remaining sureties), and when the second surety became insolvent, her 25% was reallocated among the remaining two sureties
(one-half to each of the remaining two sureties, leaving each of them
to bear 37.5% of the original principal obligation). *See above* §23(b).
This analysis is arguably unfair to the remaining sureties, however.
Had the creditor not released the first surety until *after* the second surety
had become insolvent (and the virile shares had already been reallocated,
one-third to each of three solvent sureties), the creditor would have released the first surety's 33% virile share, rather than 25%, as before
(leaving only 66% to be reallocated upon the second surety's insolvency,
only 33% to each of the remaining two sureties). Should the creditor
not bear the entire actual burden of having released a surety, regardless
of the timing of the another surety's insolvency? The law is not clear on
this point, but comment (d) to Civil Code article 1803 (governing the
parallel concept of remission of solidary obligors) reports that prominent French doctrine would have the creditor bear part of the insolvency
loss; i.e., the amount the creditor had released earlier would be retroactively recalculated upon the second surety's later insolvency. These comments, while not "law," are certainly very persuasive authority, so one
would expect the courts to follow the retroactive-recalculation approach
suggested by the French doctrine. Only time will tell.

(c) Defenses Specific to the Surety

In addition to asserting whatever defenses the principal obligor
might have had (except lack of capacity or discharge in bankruptcy),
the surety might be able to assert certain "suretyship defenses." These
defenses protect the surety from behavior by the creditor that changes
the surety's situation for the worse. The effect of these defenses differs depending upon the type of suretyship arrangement. This section will outline the three types of suretyship arrangements and then
discuss the suretyship defenses.

(1) Three Types of Suretyship

The law identifies three kinds of suretyship arrangements: legal,
commercial, and ordinary. Civ. C. art. 3041. Each suretyship

arrangement is categorized according to the type of obligation guaranteed and the source and terms of the suretyship contract. This book will address only the latter two categories, as "legal" suretyship arises pursuant to separate specific legislation, regulation, or court order. Civ. C. art. 3043.

A suretyship is "commercial" if one of three conditions is met: (1) the surety is engaged in a suretyship business (e.g., a bonding company); (2) either the surety or the principal obligor is a business entity (e.g., a corporation, partnership, or LLC); or (3) either the principal obligation or the suretyship contract arises out of a "commercial transaction" of the principal obligor or the surety, respectively. Civ. C. art. 3042. The law does not supply a definition for the term "commercial transaction," which makes the definition of a "commercial suretyship" somewhat circular. As a general guide, substitute the term "business deal" for "commercial transaction." The sense here is that the cause of the arrangement from the obligor's perspective must be more about making money (commerce) than about supporting a personal, family, or household (consumer) purpose.

An "ordinary" suretyship is thus the exceptional, residual category, encompassing only unremunerated, family- or friendship-oriented arrangements in which individuals stand behind other individuals to support domestic goals. A parent guaranteeing a child's personal car loan, for example, might qualify as an "ordinary" suretyship, although if the car is to be used in the child's business, this would likely push the transaction into the realm of "commercial" suretyship. Incidentally, the immediate impact of a designation of suretyship as "ordinary" as opposed to "commercial" is that an ordinary suretyship contract is strictly construed in favor of the surety. Civ. C. art. 3044. Commercial suretyship contracts are construed like any other commercial contract, with no suretyship-specific presumptions to aid either side.

(2) Suretyship Defenses

The nature of the suretyship also controls the effect of each of the two defenses available specifically and exclusively to sureties. *See* Civ.

C. art. 3062. These defenses arise from the creditor's modification of the guaranteed principal obligation, and from the creditor's impairment of any real security rights in the principal obligor's property that the creditor might have in addition to the personal security right against the surety.

Modification of the guaranteed obligation might occur if, for example, the creditor prefers to negotiate with the defaulting principal obligor rather than suing or pursuing the surety right away. For example, the creditor might agree to extend the time for payment, probably in exchange for an increase in the accruing interest rate. On the one hand, the surety might not care about this—indeed, the surety might welcome such a modification of the original obligation if it means that the principal obligor will ultimately manage to pay and the surety will not have to do so. On the other hand, though, a modification might also inure to the surety's detriment. For example, any increase in the interest rate payable on the principal obligation increases the amount the surety might have to pay later on. Moreover, if the creditor grants the principal obligor an extension of time to pay, and by the time the extension runs out, the principal obligor has become insolvent or otherwise judgment-proof, the extension might have deprived the surety of the ability to recover reimbursement from the principal obligor (had the creditor pursued the surety immediately, rather than extending the principal obligation, the surety might have collected from the principal obligor before she became insolvent). *See above* § 23(a).

Impairment of real security occurs when, for example, the creditor fails to file a UCC-1 financing statement to perfect an Article 9 security interest (or fails to properly record or reinscribe a mortgage) that encumbers the principal obligor's property and secures the principal obligation. This failure prejudices the real security rights in the principal obligor's property (collateral) by making the security interest or mortgage unenforceable against third parties with competing interests in the property. *See above* §§ 3, 11. As a result of the creditor's "impairment of collateral," the surety's right to step into the creditor's shoes and exercise the creditor's real security rights by subrogation, *see above* § 23(a)(2), has also been potentially impaired.

The law seeks to protect the surety from either of these adverse effects of the creditor's actions. If a *material* modification is made to the principal obligation *without the surety's advance consent,* or if the creditor impairs any real security rights securing that obligation, the suretyship obligation is affected in one of two ways, depending upon the nature of the suretyship. An *ordinary* suretyship is extinguished, but a *commercial* suretyship is extinguished only to the extent that the modification or impairment actually prejudices the surety (and not at all in the rare case in which the principal obligation is not for payment of money, and the surety should have foreseen such a change in the ordinary course). For example, a commercial surety will be released from the obligation to guarantee any renegotiated additional interest beyond what would have accrued on the original obligation (if the renegotiation occurs without the surety's consent). As for impairment of collateral, if the surety does not have to resort to the creditor's real security rights to collect from the principal obligor, or if no third parties have competing interests in the collateral, for example, failure to perfect or record a security interest or mortgage will not likely have actually prejudiced the surety, so such impairments might well not present a defense to the surety. The creditor bears the burden of showing the extent to which any modification or impairment has not prejudiced a commercial surety. Civ. C. art. 3062.

(d) Waiver of Defenses

Because suretyship is fundamentally a matter of contract, the surety can waive in the contract the right to assert otherwise available defenses. Civ. C. art. 3040. Suretyship defenses (and any defenses of the principal obligor) clearly can be and often are waived in commercial suretyship agreements, and the effectiveness of such waivers is largely uncontroversial.

The controversial question is whether the "defenses" relating to *remission* (release) of the principal obligor or other sureties under Civil Code article 1892 can be waived. Can a surety agree (in advance) to remain liable even if the principal obligor is released? Would this not undermine an important protective purpose of the law? It is quite clear that the creditor cannot undermine the law simply by "reserving rights" against the surety when it releases the principal obligor—such reservation (actually, a waiver by the surety of the effect of release of the obligor) must be in the suretyship agreement if it is to be effective at all. The comment to Civil Code art. 3040 seems to accept the possibility of contractual waiver even of the release rules, although it suggests that such a contract might not be a "suretyship" contract as a result. Ultimately, it is unclear whether the provisions regarding release of a surety upon release of the principal obligor or another surety set up a public policy rule or simply a suppletive rule. Perhaps these provisions are suppletive and variable by contract for *commercial* sureties, but binding public policy imperatives for *ordinary* sureties. Resolution of this question will have to await further judicial application.

§25 Termination

Some suretyship arrangements are for one obligation only, and such agreements generally terminate when the principal obligation is extinguished. Civ. C. art. 3059. In contrast, many commercial suretyship arrangements, in particular, are "continuing guarantees," in which the surety agrees to guarantee *future* indebtedness. The surety can terminate a guarantee of future debt and avoid liability on obligations incurred after termination by providing notice of termination to the creditor. A termination notice does *not* absolve the surety of liability for guaranteed obligations that the creditor has extended (or is bound to extend) to the principal obligor before the creditor receives notice of termination, however. Civ. C. art. 3061. Similarly, a termination notice may not prejudice the creditor or principal obligor if they have changed their position in detrimental reliance on the existence of the suretyship. If the creditor learns that the surety has died, that qualifies as notice of termination, as well, releasing the surety's succession from liability for any future obligations, unless a universal successor unequivocally confirms—orally or in writing—the suretyship obligation.

Index